This work, in any part or in its entirety, is the intellectual property of the authors listed and may not be reprinted or used in any fashion whatsoever without the express written consent of the author(s).

20 November, 2016

Forward

It has been my extreme honour and pleasure to collaborate on a subject with Maria Wheatley. Maria is a tireless researcher, having devoted the whole of her life to the studies of scared water, dowsing, megaliths and esoterica. She has been 'boots on the ground' on all of these subjects and so her research and opinion carry great weight.

Early in the writing, it became clear to me that she and would not necessarily agree on everything and that is only to the good. The reader will be then even more of an active participant in the soul discussion surrounding these topics and that is just as it should be.

This particular edition pleases me greatly as it represents a gift from my colleague Maria to myself during an interesting part of my life. I also want to acknowledge the kind contribution of James Swager on his discussions of Newgrange. Thank you, James

Each chapter of this book…at least my part…begins with the same reminder.

Cara St.Louis
Heronsgate November 2016

The Invitation

Once upon a time there was a German IT specialist, a Russian astronomer and mathematician, an Austrian physicist, a Slavic archaeological researcher and videographer, a Japanese doctor of alternative medicine, and an American writer. Although they had not made each other's actual acquaintance, they were all hurtling pell-mell for the same point in time and space: the return of the race known as the Fae. The American writer was befriended by an English scholar of the ancient Sacred Sites. Certainly they do not all agree about everything. However, the common threads run like pure and unbreakable gold through all their work. All of the people were assembled, by virtue of the writer's keyboard, each bringing a piece of a glorious puzzle and an invitation toward discovery was extended. Is it even possible to decline such a dazzling and spectacular summons? Not for me.

This book isn't just the result of my receiving one at a time the outlines of individual programs in place, which unfolded clearly and undeniably, but with that I was allowed to glimpse potent and fruitful research that added substance and context to the issues. In the end, what I felt I had been given was a complete presentation of the truth of the human condition.

It seems to me quite clear that we have all been asking the same fundamental questions. Why does it seem that our environment in total has the effect of pushing us down instead of lifting us up?

Why does it seem that life gets worse, more tiresome, with fewer victories and the victories we do gain are hollow and deeply unsatisfying? Why is our health slipping away? How are we becoming more and more isolated from the earth on which we live, from each other and from our own inner wisdom? Why are there no answers to our questions in our caches of wisdom and history? In other words, it begins with the simple observation that things just aren't right and we see the effects on ourselves and our children and, hopefully, we then really start to dig. Why do we see ourselves as powerless victims? All of the segments of our lives as we examine them reveal what can only be characterized as an all-out assault on humanity. Once we start to understand the methods of assault such as the multi-faceted effects of the aerosol war, transhumanism via nanoparticles in the air and in vaccines, altering our food such that our bodies literally have an allergic reaction to what we eat and drink...once we let that settle then we turn to the Who and the Why.

These critical areas of investigation, which have not only to do with our survival and ability to think but also with that of our children and any potential future generations, tend to lead – at least for me – to an analysis of how we became entities who could be manipulated so very easily and thoroughly. That led to a real investigation and understanding of the education process since about the beginning of the 19th century and the role of behavioural studies in commandeering our free will and energy. By now, one might be asking, what has any of this to do with the Return of the Fae? The answer is: everything. The entire idea is to make us Forget.

Forget what? Forget that a terrifically advanced civilization lies just a few centuries behind us. Forget that it was peopled with our ancestors, a race ancient and mighty and magical. If there is any sort of 'missing link,' this is it.

Why is there, even now, such an all-out effort to control our thinking, minds, memories and imaginations? The answer is likely two-fold. First, it is important that we have been removed from any sort of context, that we have no way of comparing the 'before' to the 'now.' We have been convinced over a few generations that we are helpless, unable to function in any way without our Overlords. The second part of the answer, though, has to do with the enormous amount of energy and resources that are levelled at us at all times in order to try to keep us 'under control.' It is curious indeed that stabling us requires untold amounts of manoeuvring, time, energy, and resources. Yet, for all that, we continue to leak out of our conformity suits. After we consider the who and the why and the tools of subjugation, after we learn to control the horror of that realization, we really must ask why does it take so much concentrated effort to distract and immobilize us? One can only conclude that human beings must actually be quite powerful and naturally sovereign beings. Since several generations of us now have been bred and led to believe that we are weaklings, sheep in need of a shepherd, it becomes very important to try to determine in what ways we are so powerful that an all-out assault is necessary to keep us under control. Additionally, it is not just us under malicious attack. It is also our home. The air, the soil, the water, the seed…these fundamental aspects of our beautiful planet are being destroyed or changed in very significant ways either to assist in changing us without our consent or to assist in disempowering the planet itself, also without our consent. These things are self-evident in observation. If we can remember why we are so powerful it takes a space age armada to manage us, then we can break free. I think we can break free easily.

So it seems imperative then that we really have a look at who we are in light of the full spectrum dominance assault upon us. It was this question that led me to the perception shattering understanding of our ancestry. We need to remember who we are in light of the brutal attempt to change us, damage us, hamstring us, and weaken both our memory and the ability to reason effectively. If we were simply cannon fodder or useless eaters it would be a small matter to eliminate most if not all of us permanently. So why keep us alive and in such numbers? Well, the simplest answer seems to be we have someone they want.

Who is *they*? The simplest answer to that, for now, is that we have a predator. Our predator is parasitic in nature and feeds off our energy. This is a theory to which I subscribe because I think the evidence is overwhelming that this is the case. However, I also believe that we have at least one tool that the predator does not have. We have our Imagination as the translator between what is in the morphogenic field, which has been called pure potential, and the material plane in which we live. We are, in fact, magical creatures. One of the clues that we have our own brand of magic is that we are surrounded by our own creations, which struggle to visibly manifest in an environment that is hostile to anything enlivened or authentic. Yet somehow we manage. If we can think of it…imagine it…it can become a physical reality. The other clue is that we are, in fact, surrounded by dark magic set loose often and in quantity to quell our free movement. Who the parasite is and where It or They came from really is something we can try to answer in this book. The answer stems from the evidence of who WE are. *The Predator is who we are not*. That sounds ambiguous and airy-fairy, if you'll forgive my use of that term in this context, but as we shall see, it is not.

In fact, it was by virtue of studying very precise investigative results from several sources, that I was set firmly on this path. The first real evidence came from a German scientist, a man called Erhard Landmann, who was an IT specialist for Siemens. Landmann, who is at the time of this writing in his eighties, began to put a name to what actually could truly be called a missing link. In fact, we can only call it missing because the memory or history of it has been deliberately erased from our consciousness. This entity, this missing piece I am bringing has been maligned and belittled and hidden and changed until it is no longer recognizable. I speak here of the Fae, a powerful, noble and germinal entity on this planet.

Landmann himself is and was something of a John Nash-type character, a brilliant man who sees the patterns in words. He began making etymological associations that seemed to indicate a real presence of a race which could be called the Fae. The evidence mounted until the fact of the Fae became undeniable. The word, Fae, is a very old word. It is well known in Ireland. The term simply became elongated and mystified and, in the 20th century, denigrated, to the term 'fairy.' Once he began earnestly seeing the etymological evidence of a very bold and meaningful race and what amounts to a foundational influence, then the evidence became massive and convincing and he felt compelled to write and lecture about it.

Landmann has also located the Fae as extra-terrestrial and has excellent evidence that this race came from outside our solar system and, in fact, from which planet they have come. In that case, we have a race from another world who became our seed race and most magical ancestor. This race, based on my research, found a way to wed themselves to the earth in ways we no longer understand, became guardians of the inner earth energies both in water and frequency, and bequeathed to us a history and birthright that was still manifesting itself in ancient sites, art and beauty up until just a few centuries ago.

Etymological evidence is accepted as standard scientific research and the basis for many good conclusions about culture, about migration, and about ancestry. Aside from this, however, we will have a good look at the oral histories and the so-called Bardic Tales which bring a history to life that is tantalizingly close to what could be called a 'Tale of the Fae'. The questions of who the Fae were (or are) and where they were (or are) are critical if we are going to suggest…and we are…that they are, in fact, the Seed Race of Humanity on this planet.

Not only is there extremely good evidence that the Fae are our primary ancestors but it would seem there is important evidence that a race capable of constructing cities and monuments was functioning in full glory as recently as just a few centuries ago. This is where the Slavic investigator and videographer, Sylvie Ivanowa, appears as part of what I have named the 'team.' Here I find it useful to insert a short piece written by Greg Carlwood and used with his permission in a volume I wrote on the False Chronology to try to help summarize the thrust of an amazing body of work by this woman.

"…a lot of us are open to the idea that there was an ancient advanced culture…Atlantis or Hyperborea perhaps…and maybe these seeders of knowledge were Caucasian-looking people from these civilizations. Maybe they were escaping the destruction of their own culture from these parasites or maybe natural disasters, as well…maybe they spread out and integrated into less advanced cultures to spread knowledge and rebuild their world, a struggle they've been having ever since. Maybe this was a back and forth that was finally laid to rest with the Reformation and the European expansion, and the Inquisition and Colonialism and the Spanish conquests. Is it possible that these could have all been aspects of one campaign? Could it be that something more epic and not so distant was hidden away over that period of time? Could the genie have been put back in the bottle just a few hundred years ago? Is a campaign of this magnitude feasible? What happened to the psychedelic basis for religion in ancient times? What happened to the megalithic sites? (It is possible that there was) a radically recent cataclysm which would explain how a parasitic elite could dominate humanity and put us in such a position of servitude and ignorance as we are in today."[1]

Researcher Sylvie Ivanowa has gathered an extraordinary body of data that strongly suggests there was a very advanced civilization operating on this planet up to just a few hundred years ago. She has visited countless ancient sacred sites and made detailed investigations as to whether the archaeological evidence is in line with the common cultural tales of the people living in the area during the time when these sites were erected. Most of the time, the two things do not line up. When we think about that possibility, that the common history of some of these sites is erroneous, we have to wonder who is hiding what and why? Part and parcel of the attempt to completely obscure recent human history leads to the next expert on the 'team,' Dr. Anatoly Fomenko.

Dr. Anatoly Fomenko is a mathematician, statistician and astronomer of the highest calibre teaching at the University of Moscow. He and what is by now a team in the hundreds have verified that it is quite likely that hundreds and hundreds of years have been added to the consensual timeline…that is to say, history as we know it. During the phantom years, several pretenders to thrones across Europe appeared and laid claim to territory. Many of the characters through which we trace our lineage and justify our

---

[1] https://www.youtube.com/watch?v=sgje5d5APTA   When The Atlantis Survivors Wake Up.

actions, such as Charlemagne, appear to be fictions. Rome is actually much closer to us in time than we think it is. The fact of Rome and subsequently the Vatican, especially as it pertains to the altered timeline, becomes extremely important to our discussion. For our purposes now, however, it is simply important to demonstrate that a significant portion of our history is a complete fabrication.[2] To a certain extent it will be necessary to prove this within the text here. However, this is being offered as a largely unknown in the English speaking world phenomenon which lends credence to the idea that something is being hidden. Combined with Ivanowa's work, we seem to have a very recent society or race or culture or all of the above hidden from our modern knowledge. The evidence is very suggestive and alarming. It is always worth noting when writing about the chronology that the consensual chronology has been under aggressive challenge by non-English speaking Europe for centuries. Indeed, the very last contribution made by Isaac Newton before he died was a book challenging what he considered to be a timeline that was an utter fabrication.

Next, who wants to hide it and why?

I did mention so-called dynasties that appeared during a certain period after 900 AD. The new chronology, commissioned by Pope Gregory in the 16th century, established and reinforced these dynasties which, by and large, still rule globally. Were they to stay in power there would need to be no alternative claimants. There

---

[2] For more on this go to either my work, St.Louis, C. *Workbook Episode One: The False Chronology* or the primary source by Fomenko, A. *History, Fiction or Science.*

would need to be a population willing to accept them and their power and control. There are extraordinary facts that seem to make no sense in light of the size and need of world population, for example, such as the fact that Queen Elizabeth of England owns fully one-sixth of the land mass of the earth. How did that happen and why is it acceptable to the other 7 billion inhabitants? The structures of individual power and security would have to be eroded on the one hand and the indoctrination in the lies would need to be implemented on the other. This we have seen without question since 1818 and the introduction of certain schooling systems, mandatory schooling, and specialization in the workplace.[3] The addition of behaviour modification techniques in the workplace and, most importantly, in the schools fast-forwarded the erosion. The nuclear family would need to come under attack and parents' places in family life would need to be rendered laughable to children and society (remember the 1960s?). All in all, this applied system would create a vacuum individually and collectively which could readily be filled by schools, military, governments and so forth. In these ways could our very recent ancestors be relegated to anonymity and our new masters be reinforced. The behaviour modification has been so thorough, in fact, that we literally thank our masters for their control.

And, yet…the melancholy, the unhappiness, the restlessness, the dissatisfaction…it is with us and growing. On the one side we have a humanity crippled, hobbled, fundamentally unhappy. We grow ill due to the actual biological aspects of our control which

---

[3] St.Louis, C. *Dangerous Imagination, Silent Assimilation.*

come to us through the air, via the aerosol war euphemistically termed geoengineering, the addition of chemicals and nanoparticles to our cells via the same, we hurtle toward becoming part machine with the advent of the transhumanist 'future,' all of which is meant somehow to separate us from our birthright as human beings. The food we eat causes illness and what amount to allergic reactions. The soil is raped and destroyed and made sterile. Seeds have become self-terminating and so do not recreate life. And our water is under all-out assault all of the time. Oil spills are just the beginning. Dr. Masaru Emoto, a groundbreaking researcher into the relationship of human beings and water, demonstrated that water carries information. It carries emotion and, in fact, water is the carrier of our memory. That postulate is not too much of a stretch given Emoto's work. In our bodies (75% or more water) or on the earth (71% of the earth's surface), it is sacred water that holds the planetary memory,,,currently being destroyed by fracking. In fact, destruction of the sentient being that is water is the true purpose of fracking. Water also holds the secret to true energy, in the form of vortex and levitation mechanics, which is another very important component of our arsenal to bury.

Additionally, more very good research from Germany comes from Austrian physicist Wolfgang Wiedergut.[4] He was originally a free energy researcher who studied at the Technical University in Vienna. However, his studies, as with so much of physics research, led toward the esoteric and metaphysical. He was an expert in the

---

[4] http://bindu.ufo.at/

Vedic Scriptures and the energy research of Tesla, Schauberger, Reich and Russell. Unfortunately, this man died of cancer some years ago and quite young, at that. The piece of his research that makes its way into this discussion has to do with his astonishing work on vortexes. He analyses the idea of frequency in connection with the ley lines in interesting ways. The connection simply cannot be discounted. Could this be, as some including myself suspect, a communication from the earth itself or perhaps from the guardians of such? Could it be an attempt to apply healing to a fractured earth frequency so very brutal and overwhelming since the beginning of the 20th century? There are important examples of divine feminine energy being supplanted, minimized and muted by the technology of the 20th century in much the same way churches were installed atop natural energy centres in the thousand years prior. The idea is to suppress, use and alter what is natural for unnatural purposes. Clamp it down, shut it up, modify any expression of energy.

It is also very important to note that this book does not present a saviour race, come back to help us avoid the end. In fact, this book supports the idea that the Fae existed as our seed race here on earth and are the source of our ancestral strength and magic. This book supports deeply the notion that the Fae have been brought again to a level of consciousness which has not been for some time because the planet is under such base attack. It is their job, if you will, to tend the Apple Tree and we, the apples, will benefit mightily from their concerted ministrations.

We have a parasitic predator that thinks in terms of eons and centuries. Human beings are not like that: we are agile, adaptable, fluid, light on our feet. Whereas our enemy is plodding but deep, we are quick and nimble. We are also powerful and magical. Our imagination and the use of it lies at the base of every attack and every triumph. If the Fae were our seed race, then we have access to everything we have inherited from this ancestor. We tend to get information that suggests we are weak and we don't have the capacity to do much. Hence, machines are developed to 'assist' us. The reality is that all machines, *all machines*, are dim copies of human capacities. It is this ability, unique in the universe, which makes us a prize among prizes. It is this we inherit from the Fae. It is this, in each and every one of us that will save us.

Now, as the writer having a look at the gathering of research and information, all of which we will discuss in some measure, I should introduce the woman I met who is a master dowser and scholarly researcher of the sacred sites in Britain and Europe. Maria Wheatley brought to my attention during the time when I was gathering this yeasty mixture that there is such a thing as the Celtic Heart. Writer John Lash calls it the Celtic Heart(h). Just about the time we started to discuss this idea that there is an origin for the Celts as such, I was made aware of the massive amount of oral history in Ireland on the peoples who have been there. There is, apparently, no creation myth associated with Ireland but rather a long series of invasion stories. *Ireland, Land of the Pharaohs*[5] was a

---

[5]Power, A. *Land of the Pharaohs.*

brilliant beginning to my understanding of the magic that began and continues in Ireland.

Naturally, Ireland is not the only Celtic centre in the world. I have had important and interesting experiences in Brittany and Scotland. When one considers this idea that there is a starting point for the Celtic race and that we have very good evidence that an ancient race called the Fae is a seed race for all of humanity, it is logical to see these things as connected. Yes, these things converge. One of the places to feast with the most meat on its bones turns out to be the Battle of Moytura in Sligo. It is known as the First Battle. There we see for the first time a Good Fairy and a Bad Fairy and, I believe, the bad fairies chased the good fairies across time and space and eons and this is one long campaign, in which we find ourselves today. The turmoil, the death and destruction, are the ever-present evidence of one long campaign begun at the time of the First Battle.

Finally, we have a lively discussion of the living nature of Sacred Water and an in-depth description of the Sacred Sites left behind by Maria Wheatley and with a contribution from expert James Edward Swager. Maria focuses her discussion on the Sidhe, and their relationship to the sacred sites. As I said, this journey for me has been an invitation impossible to refuse.

Chapter One – It's All About the Context

We have our Imagination as the translator between what is in the morphogenic field, which has been called pure potential, and the material plane in which we live. We are, in fact, magical creatures.

About teaching history: one of the things I also am is a Waldorf teacher. In the United Kingdom, this is known as a Steiner teacher. Our pedagogy and child development paradigms were given to us by an Austrian philosopher called Dr. Rudolf Steiner. He developed this form of schooling in 1919 saying that if we did not change the way we educated our children, well, it was all over for us. It seems his opinion was a good one. All will become clear in a moment.

In Waldorf schools, we believe the child is incarnating, year by year, into this particular lifetime. We teach them history by recapitulating it, in the order of appearance, with each school year having its own theme...the next theme in line from beginning to now. Based on the idea that the Fae, or fairy, was an actual separate race all but lost to the mists of time, perhaps it will come as no surprise that first grade (class one) revolves around the fairy tales. In almost all others styles of education, history is taught in a fragmented way. I used to think of it as self-aggrandizing, meant to create soldiers, and that is true. However, fragmented history and only knowing about one's own part of the world does not allow us to solve the mystery of who we are and where we come from. I began teaching many, many years before I understood about the Fae and I was always a bit confused as to why we started with fairy tales. However, I certainly understand it now. It was the First Race. Rudolf Steiner has said the following:

"Fairy tales are never thought out [i.e., invented]; they are the final remains of ancient clairvoyance, experienced in dreams by human beings who still had the power.

Rudolf Steiner, ON THE MYSTERY DRAMAS
(Rudolf Steiner Press, 1983), p. 93.

"Among them were many who had preserved in large measure the heritage of the old dim clairvoyance — the intermediate state between waking and sleeping. Such men knew the spiritual world from their own experience and could tell their fellow-men of what goes on there. In this way there arose a world of stories about spiritual beings and events.
The fairy-tales and sagas of the peoples came originally from these real experiences in the spirit."

Rudolf Steiner, ESOTERIC SCIENCE - AN
OUTLINE
(Rudolf Steiner Press, 1969), p. 219.

As a slight digression, I would like to state here that someone recently asked me how the Aboriginals might factor into this Fae tale. The Australian Aboriginals still live in Dream Time. Some say it will be the end of them. Regardless, it seems that these types of cultures are prime candidates for the in-between consciousness states between the original Fae and modern man. They would then be rare and exquisitely important. They could probably tell us just what happened. Therefore, I will be discussing one unique quality of the Aboriginals when we arrive at that chapter dealing with frequency.

Back to the plan, though. I have decided that the best way to 'incarnate' this knowing into the reader's consciousness is simply to do what I know works: start at the beginning. That means, I think, that I must split up Landmann's work which is both etymological in nature and points all the way back to an alien race. The arrival of such a race would have to coincide or precede, according to my research, the Battle of Moytura. Landmann contends, I believe, that this race has been visiting the earth over the course of all the centuries. For the purposes of identifying the Fae Race and where they made their first documented stand, this is not important, at least not yet. We are trying to identify that very place. We could call it the Celtic Heart(h) or we may find that is somewhere even further back in time or even on a different planet. But one must decide where to start and take the plunge and, most importantly, stay the course! One cannot be distracted by every butterfly that flutters past. That is a real pitfall that leads nowhere. It seems clear that we should wed one thing to another or at least present them as *original context* for consideration. It is also quite likely that the visual evidence still scattered thickly across the earth should come into this original discussion. It is there we may visit both the archaeologist and the scholar of sacred sites.

First, consider the Bardic Tale that is known as the Battle of Moytura. According to the modern Bard, Robin Williamson, this take only exists in two manuscripts: one is in Old Irish and the other in Middle Irish. It is a fact that even the Irish people I know for the most part had never heard of this tale. I have heard it referred to as the First Tale, the First Battle and it is, by Bardic accounts, the closest thing in Irish culture to a creation myth. It is a "compendium of ancient Irish magical lore."[6]

According to the very beginning of this tale, there was a people inhabiting the area known as Ireland eons before what we might call modern man. They were known as the Fir Bolg. They were called this, the People of the Leather Bag, because they each carried a leather bag out of which they created the Four Seas. Four is an exceptionally important number in these and future tales. After the Fir Bolg had created Ireland by the sweat of their brow, there appeared either over the sea or from under the sea, a race called the Fomorans. The bardic tale describes them thusly: they had one eye with which to covet, one arm with which to grasp and one leg with which to invade. The story is that they eventually did away with the Fir Bolg. To me, this may well be a landing story. Since they are

---

[6] Williamson, R. https://www.youtube.com/watch?v=X_7OmYLjLlE

described from coming across the sea, the question is from where? There is also an idea they came from under the sea...this could be literal or it could be a subconscious description of the unknown. In the widest view, it could be a description of the change between the end of Lemuria and the beginning of Atlantis. I do lean toward the idea that it was a landing story but not the first landing. The Fomorans certainly do come off as the Bad Guys (Bad Fairies?). There were four kings of the Fomorans. One of the kings had a 'baleful' eye, which he kept covered with a brass cover, a leather cover and a lead cover. This was one dangerous eye. Or was it actually an eye? What we can say is that it was a weapon located on or in his head. That I think we can say. Whatever that eye beheld would in that moment be 'turned to stone.'

The story goes on that the Fir Bolg were enslaved by the Fomorans and had to pay a tax to them. The tax was paid each Halloween and included two-thirds of the corn, the milk, and the children to be used as slaves. This sort of activity tends to lead me away from the idea that this tale describes the transition between Lemuria and Atlantis and really toward the idea that this was a hostile alien landing.

According to the bardic tale, the Tuatha de Danaan existed at the same time. They were known as the People of Art (Magic) and Skill. They had learned their knowledge and power in the Four Cities of Instruction...the city of the stone, the city of the spear, the city of the sword and the city of the cauldron. (Interestingly, in the Norse mythologies a cauldron also figures quite prominently in their

creation tales and some have speculated that it represents the larynx.)
They did have a king but they also had a Chief Druid known as the
All Father (another mirror of the Norse myths). The Tuatha de
Danaan decided they would take Ireland for their own for they came
from the Four Cities of Instruction, yes, but these were in a
'universe' near this one. In the tale, they are not native to this planet
at all. They sailed in 'special ships' to the land of Erin and landed on
1 May. It is said when they landed they 'burned their boats upon the
shore.' This is a piece for which I have yet to find meaning unless it
was simply a statement of never intending to return from whence
they came. The conversation appears to indicate that they arrived on
a cloud or in a three day storm of mist and smoke. Again, this is
likely an interstellar landing story in my view.

They also engaged the Fir Bolg in battle. So if we look at
what is written here, we have the Creators of the island of Erin
between two landing entities. The Fomorans are ruthlessly negative,
at least for the Fir Bolg, and appear to have a mighty weapon. They
have come from 'over the sea' or 'under the sea.' The Tuatha de
Danaan have come from outer space. This is clearly stated in the
tale. Pity the poor Fir Bolg!

In this battle that waged between the Fir Bolg and the Tuatha
de Danaan, the Fir Bolg gained the upper hand right away,
slaughtering many and wounding the king. They had severed his arm
from his body. However, the Tuatha de Danaan were then led by
their Chief Druid, also known as the All Father, who managed to
turn the battle in their favour. The Fir Bolg were given a small

territory in the west of Ireland and the islands of the sea such as Aran
and Mann, and were banished to the same.

Meanwhile the Great Healer of the Tuatha de Danaan made a
new arm for the king, an arm made of silver. It was flawlessly
perfect as a replica of a real arm and moved just the same. Despite
what we might think of this new metal arm and how we could
classify something like that today (transhumanism?), the man was
still considered unfit to be king. A new king was selected called
Bres, who was half Fomoran and half Tuatha De Danaan. This came
about as the end-product of what appears to be a rape by a Fomoran
King of the daughter of a T de D king. The Fomoran king gave the
mother of Bres a golden ring to give to him at the right time.

There is much to say here about this Battle and I will.
However, I must interject here to say that I wonder if this tale has
been fulfilled yet or if it is just now beginning to be fulfilled? When
I listen to a bard recount the tale of the Battle of Moytura, and I
listen to the details of the second battle, it seems to me that it is a tale
of the freezing of the Fae, who are the Tuatha de Danaan certainly,
and the return of their strength, power and life still approaches.

I believe another very useful way to look at this story, one
that will crack open our perception and the potential information
lying within it, is to re-present it with some simplifications. I will
summarize it at some point using such terms as Good Fairy and Bad
Fairy and so forth. I do believe that the basis of this long battle, this
long campaign, and this long trial can be located quite squarely here
in the tale of The Battle of Moytura. Furthermore, I do not believe

that the events of this tale are over and done with but rather are the on-going epic battle in which we find ourselves.

However, we cannot use it as a tool until we lay out what is vital. Bres was the name of the King who was half Fomoran and half Tuatha de Danaan. He inherited his father's Fomoran greediness in the extreme. As a result he was profoundly unpopular and was deposed. In his place was put the old king, the one whose arm had been severed. The silver replacement was regrown as an actual flesh and bone arm by a very skilled healer.

The golden ring was given to Bres by his mother, they stole as many of the Tuatha de Danaan riches as they could get away with and as well as the harp of the High Druid, the All Father. This harp is critical. They made their way to the father of Bres who recognized him because of the golden ring. The Evil King, father of Bres, offered to keep the Druid's Harp but sent him to Balor of the Baleful Eye, the king with the weapon, to raise an army against the Tuatha de Danaan. His Fomoran father promised to hide the harp in a place where the Druid would never find it. To me, this says simply that the Druids (the old magic) cannot release the Fae.

This magical harp drove the cycle of the seasons. In other words, it would have controlled the whole and natural cycle of time for the Tuatha de Danaan. In fact, the seasons would have meant the entire birth-death cycle, the planting and harvesting, and so forth. In fact, when the Fomoran king received this harp, the seasons stopped and the 'world' was plunged into a frozen, endless, grey February. FE-bruary. Did, in fact, the Bad Fairies capture and hide from the

Good Fairies their destiny? This in itself is an esoteric crime of the highest order. This may well be when the Fae decided to wed themselves to the planet but we shall examine that as we proceed.

Balor of the Baleful Eye, the king who would help raise an army against the Tuatha de Danaan, was the wearer of a prophecy…that he could only be killed by his own grandson. Balor had a beautiful daughter, whom he locked away in a copper tower. A Tuatha de Danaan prince got into the tower by means of a cloak of concealment and he and the daughter conceived a son, who was then named Lugh or Lugh of the Long Hand, Lugh All Skilled. He was so called because he possessed every skill. He was raised with the Tuatha de Danaan and not with his Fomoran mother. To me, this would seem to be the arrival of the first true human, for each human being is all-skilled when left to grow up unmolested and unfettered by the false construct in which we languish.

Lugh met one day, in concert with the Norse myths once again, three women clothed completely in black feathers. In the Norse myths or even in the play Macbeth, these are known as the Norns or the witches. They often represent past, present and future. With the Druid's harp frozen and concealed then these three would indeed be the location of time and destiny. They handed him the Spear of Destiny and told him he was the only one fit to rule Tara at this time.

He took the spear. He took the destiny. And he took the road to Tara.

In fact, it may be important to point out now that the Norse myths came long after the Fairies. The cauldron of the Norse Norns is sometimes viewed as the larynx, as I mentioned, which is in some esoteric circles seen as the modus operandi for manifesting life and life's trappings into this world. It is by sound and by the human voice that the imagination is most powerfully used and it is in the oral histories that much is preserved and defended. The High Druid also possessed a cauldron which seems to have passed out of his control at some point. Perhaps it is the case that the Druid's Harp, concealed and frozen, is the Celtic Heart? If so, this is what needs rescuing. We shall continue to investigate.

It is also very important to note that when Lugh approached Tara, he met a gatekeeper and it was only when he demonstrated to the gatekeeper that he, Lugh, one man, possessed every skill and art already present in Tara that he was allowed inside the walls. The reigning king, the one with the healed arm, handed the crown to Lugh. Once again, as I dip into my life's experience as a Waldorf teacher, I can say that the truest characterization of the human being is that a human can do anything. All of us are renaissance people, as it were, and the teacher stands before the class to try to demonstrate that each day by teaching all subjects. Without going too deeply into the pedagogical arena, I feel comfortable proposing that here in Lugh, both Fomoran and Tuatha de Danaan, we have the first human being.

Bres did not work out well as a mixture of the two entities, the product of a Fomoran father and a Tuatha de Danaan mother and a product of rape at that. Lugh was the product of a Fomoran mother and a Tuatha de Danaan father, who welcomed the union. The prophesy was that he, Lugh, would be the only one capable of 'killing the evil king with the overpowering, irresistible weapon.' Lugh, in his combination of the two entities, would kill the Original Bad Fairy. Interestingly. Lugh would also be the product of two alien races but the motive was completely different.

It is here in the tale that another character appears. Given the modern theory that not only do we have a parasitic predator but that blood sacrifices on an unprecedented scale are involved (we call them wars), it is crucial to have a long look at this character and this part of the tale.

The High Druid or All Father journeyed, as Lugh became the king and prepared for battle, to meet the Mother of All Battles, also known as The Morgue (the morgue!). She was a terrifying creature who lived alone on the banks of the River Inshin near Sligo. When the High Druid found The Morgue she was washing herself in the river and blood was flowing down the water. The High Druid wanted to know where the Fomorans would land and where they could look for battle. She told him they would land in Skenya but the battle would take place in a second location also called Moytura, near Sligo. He then asked her the price of this information.

Essentially she replied that the blood of every being slain at Moytura would be her reward. She said to him,

"I am she would stands among the fallen. I am she who knows the ways of taking
    life."

She also mentioned that she wanted the blood of the kidneys. Since the kidneys house fear, it seems that fear-filled blood was on the menu. The Morigan. The Morgue. *The Morgue*! Even in the telling of the tale, the rendition moves orally from Morgue (mor-goo) to Morigan. And the price of information and victory was a massive blood sacrifice. This also requires investigation at some point. Once again, one of the primary questions of our time is '*Who is the Predator?*' There is also always the question, how many are there? I think we will make some real progress pointing the way toward answers to those questions as we truly define who the Fae are.

As the story continues, the High Druid gets himself into trouble with the daughter of a high ranking Tuatha de Danaan. She approaches him actually then stops him in his tracks magically. That alone is astonishing. They couple and then she tries very hard to keep him from going to the battle. The question is why? Is it her love for him? Or is this a magical attempt to keep the Druid (the All Father) from participating in this battle that on the one hand is destined and on the other hand is being paid for to an auxiliary character in the form of an ungodly blood sacrifice? It is proper to remember here all the ghastly unnecessary wars which were nothing more than massive blood sacrifices, exercises in energy gathering. It is an interesting thought. In her entreaty to him not to join the battle, the woman echoes many of the features of the Faedh Fiadha, the Cry of the Deer, which is the incantation of the Fae eventually stolen by the Catholic Church.

One line of the tale reads: *Fine fighters fell there, where death was nourished.* I would like to note that as Balor of the Baleful Eye approached his grandson, Lugh, who led the Tuatha de Danaan, Lugh uttered these words:

> "*Battle come afire,*
> *Fe, Fe, Foe, Foe....*

There are a few ways to interpret this war cry but it is important to note the use of the word, Fe. Another important detail: the Druid's Harp could not be found but the Sword of Tara was recovered. This sword could answer questions put to it and it revealed the location of the Harp. Immediately the Druid reclaimed the Harp and as he began to play the natural order of the seasons returned. I still wonder, though, if this is a tale that has been told of deeds over and done with eons ago or if somehow we are still in the midst of this story, waiting for the Druid to find his Harp? It is a story of the landing of the seed race(es). It is a story of the first human being. It is a story of the first organizing of a wretched blood and fear sacrifice. There are the Norns: past, present, future and the casters of destiny. Perhaps this was just the beginning of one long campaign as the Bad Fairies chased the Good Fairies through time and space. In the end, the life of Bres was spared. Bres lived on. Bres and Lugh, both half-breeds; one good and one evil. The Druid did engage in that battle, for which he had negotiated a terrible price. I wonder what that means to us now? Was his Harp found and, if so, with all that blood on his hands could he use it? Would the magic he made with it then be pure or warped in some way? Is this also something from which the earth needs to heal and could this be why the Fae decided to wed themselves to the planet? Perhaps the decision to do so was led by the woman who tried to dissuade the Druid from joining the battle. These are simply questions flowing forth from the story of the Seed Race of the Fae.

At the end of the battle, Lugh uttered these words:

Until the stars of heaven can be counted,
Sands of the Sea
The blades of grass under hooves of horses,
The flakes of snow of every storm,
In the history of the world,
Until these shall be counted,
The dead at Moytura will never be counted at all.

I think it's still a question. Are we still in the middle of this tale?

Now that we have this incredibly important tale under our belts, another entry can be studied. "In Celtic belief men were not so much created by gods as descended from them. (For) All the Gauls assert that they are descended from Dispater, and this, they say, has been handed down to them by the Druids. Dispater was a Celtic underworld god of fertility, and the statement probably presupposes a myth, like that found among many primitive peoples, telling how men once lived underground and thence came to the surface of the earth. But it also points to their descent from the god of the underworld. Thither the dead returned to him who was ancestor of the living as well as lord of the dead"[7] Dispater as an underworld god could be little more than the Fomorans emerging from 'under the water.' …" One could say then that *we are actually a stage of the fairies' life cycle*. In over half of Europe's myths, humans came from trees whose souls are those of the fairies and deities while the rest of European myths claim that humans are descendants of a deity of the underworld. This is significant because Celtic belief holds that many fairies live within and come from the underworld as well… As Jacob Grimm points out, humans physically lie somewhere between the realms of fairies and giants." The Fomorans and the Tuatha de Danaan."

---

[7] MacCulloch, J.A. The Celtic and Scandinavian Religions, 2005

Fast forward to 1970-something. Not only does Erhard Landmann, German IT specialist, begin to join together an overwhelming amount of etymological evidence that the underlying global culture may just be something called the Fae, but for some reason he attaches it to an interest in our origins being from another planet. He finds evidence of names for other star systems and such in the Voynich Manuscripts and in the Oera Linda Book. Most of what Landmann contributed to this study will come later in a chapter dedicated to the study of words that locate the Fae here on this planet in overwhelming numbers. However, we can say that Landmann immediately attached this evidence to his curiosity about the evidence of alien abductions. He saw clearly that the thousands of tales of a woman apparition in every culture and in every time was somehow connected to the Fae. Most of his etymological research led him to really place the Fae as a female oriented race.

In this, of course, I wholeheartedly agree with him. We will examine the womanly apparitions in all cultures and ages in another chapter. However, it is important to mention, with the Battle of Moytura fresh in our minds that the good fairy, Lugh of the Long Hand, was born of a consensual and affectionate relationship between a woman of the Fomora and a man of the Tuatha de Danaan. Bres had been the product of a rape.

I believe there is an explanation for every turn of phrase that could be interpreted as an abduction by the Fae such as 'away with the fairies,' or the legends of fairies stealing children or even fetuses. (fe-tuses). My research and experience tells me that most of what is being termed alien abductions are actions conducted by the military, and that includes the UFOs of high technological evolution. And I am well aware that there is a group of military minds who have styled themselves The Avians or the Aviary whose business it has been to build a completely false overlay of aliens on this planet.[8] So to a certain extent, I will minimize this discussion of alien abductions and the more sensationalist aspects of the possibilities under consideration.

However, it is clear to me that the Fae are a real and separate race and that they come from somewhere else and they arrives eons and eons ago. What I want to add in this chapter just at the base of an analysis of the Battle of Moytura is this, directly from an article written by Landmann and translated into English. If there were any substance to the abductions of human beings by 'fairies,' which I lean away from believing, perhaps this could be traced to the bad fairies of the line of Bres. That there are bad fairies emanating from the line of Bres is a theory to which I do subscribe. It is no more unbelievable, or perhaps in some way it is the same story, than that of Cain and Abel. Eventually, one could add a consideration of the offspring of the High Druid, as well. Landmann wrote,

---

[8]http://www.bibliotecapleyades.net/esp_sociopol_aviary.htm

"Great Britain and Ireland are classical countries for traditional myths and legends of fairies, much more numerous than in any other country, despite the fact that there is no lack of these either. There are good and bad fairies. This fact is important to keep firmly in mind for further exploration of this theme. All of these stories from different cultural backgrounds yield four important clues. (*There is the number four again. Ed.*) These stand out clear and unequivocal, if we consider the Irish and British mythology, the Oera Linda Chronicle, the Voynich Manuscript and take into consideration the analysis of the languages, when examining the term "fairy" in detail.

1. Fairies are always clearly associated with space travel and UFOs, particularly in conjunction with the Galaxy "OD", "ODO", "OTI" or "OT"

2. Fairies have to do with the ancestry of mankind and their origin from space. Namely, the good fairies.

3. The evil fairies have clearly to do with the centuries-old oppression of humanity

4. Fairies are dealing with partly bizarre, weird and strange sexual incidents.

Number four is interesting, I guess, but whether or not it is true or needs to be part of this discussion remains to be seen. Come to think of it, there were some strange sexual incidents discussed in the Battle of Moytura.

In Landmann's work, however, he means the reports of people (men) being forced into sexual encounters with tall, comely, blonde aliens. Yes, we saw this scenario although the sexes were reversed in the conception of Bres. It does seem that experiencers report more than their share of these kinds of encounters. If it were a meeting with the Fae at this point, it would probably not be considered extra-terrestrial as the Fae are quite wedded to the earth. They can be seen when they want to be seen and it is reported that they interact with humans when they want to do so. While they *were* from another planet, it is utterly debatable whether or not they still come and go from there.

There is physical evidence of the location of the planet from which the Phe came, Phecda. All histories of these 'permanent visitors' lead one toward the Big Dipper (The Plough) which stands between the earth and Ursa Major. The lowest planet on the left of the cup is called PHEcda. This would come off as a mere statement were it not for the fact that the Big Dipper is circum-polar in the Northern Hemisphere. It appears to revolve around the North Star, Polaris, annually and in its tracks it forms one of the most ancient symbols existent on the earth; the swastika. It is also known as

Thor's Sigel. There again is the connection to the Norse myths. It is possible, perhaps, to try to locate the point in time when the Fae travelled here if one has a look at previous polar stars. The pole stars change within the context of the Platonic Year, every 26,000 or so years. It is also known as the precession of the equinoxes. Just before Polaris, the pole star was Kappa Draconus. One wonders if this is from when and where the Bad Fairies came? One wonders if the very probable race of reptiles operating on earth today emanated from here. Prior to that, the pole star had been Beta Ursa Minorus....the constellation in which one seems to see the dipper. Actually, this was the Pole Star, according to the astronomers from 1900 BC to 500AD. These are facts we should have at our fingertips when we dive into the next bit of evidence. However, it is not indicated that it was during this point in time that the Fae came to this planet. If anything, I would lean more toward their arrival during the last time in the precessional cycle when Polaris was our northern hemisphere pole star. Here's why.

The constellation of the Big Dipper (the Plough) appears to revolve around Polaris on an annual basis. As it does so, it forms one of the single most prevalent and ancient symbols littered across our planet: the swastika. The swastika has been until the 20th century when it and its energy were warped severely, one of most positive and hope-filled symbols we used and knew. (Remember, it is also known as Thor's Sigel another tie-in with the Norse myths). To me, it is clear that this is the calling card of the Fae.

This symbol appears in all the Americas, Europe, in China…it is truly universal and truly ancient. The warping of this symbol coincided with the application of artificial frequency overlaid on natural, feminine earth frequencies as well as the deliberate move away from using then natural musical frequency of 432 mHz. It is also a use of the principle of four, which shows up often in conjunction with the use of the number nine. This is often the case in China, for example.

Here is an excellent spot to introduce our brilliant archeaeological researcher and videographer, Sylvie Ivanowa.[9] She did very good work documenting the trail of the swastika in the history and heart of humanity. She described it as an ancient symbol of luck and harmony. I am going to include some of the most startling images of this symbol as we continue the discussion. In her work called, *Fabricated History: The Swastika*, Ivanowa begins by reminding us that in India, where the memory of what she terms The Survivors, is the strongest today, the swastika is everywhere. It finds its way into the beautiful embroidery of traditional costumes of the Slavs. Ancient Celtic stones are covered with carvings of swastikas. Swastikas find their way into the tile mosaics of the Romans. Swastikas are found on Mycenaean pottery. They appear in France and, importantly, they appear in Ireland as the Four Leaf Clover.

---

[9] https://www.youtube.com/watch?v=6RcEX6Vr56w

In Africa, they appear in Tunisia, the Sudan, Ghana, Algeria and Egypt. They are found in ancient Syria, Iran, central Asia, and South America. They have been seen as a powerful symbol of positivity all over the world. Of course, they are also a very common symbol in Native American lore and, particularly, with the Hopi tribe. The state flag of New Mexico is a stylized swastika. We will discuss the warping of the symbol, of course, when we delve into the alteration of frequency.

Native American   Brigid's Cross

Warm-hearted postcard from 1907

Additionally, for those who would argue that the *direction* in which the swastika seems to spin decides whether or not it is a symbol of good or evil, I can attest that it is displayed going both directions in many ancient cultures and often the Native Americans used it as decoration going both directions on the same article. I suppose it is possible that one direction is a nod to the good fairies and the other direction is a nod to the bad fairies. However, it could also be that when it goes both directions on a single item, perhaps it simply stands for *balance.*

The earliest consistent use of the swastika motifs in the archaeological record date to the Neolithic. The symbol appears in the Vinca Script of Neolithic Europe (Balkans, 6th-5th millennium BC). Another early attestation is on a pottery bowl found in Samarra, dated as early as 4000 BC. However, Joseph Campbell cites the use on an ornament on a late Paleolithic figurine found near Kiev (10,000 BC). This is the only known example predating Neolithic. So, when we try to decide (if we want to do so) when the Fae travelled here from Phecda, we can imagine it to be as early as 10,000 BC. That is the case if we want to accept the use of the swastika as evidence of their arrival and tenure. I do.

Particularly of interest to me were tales of Franciscan monks who got hold of the old texts (not the ancient texts, I presume, of which there were only two but of others afterward) and rewrote the history as was the task given to monks by the Pope. See the following: The Book of Invasions (Lebor Gebála Érénn compiled c.1150) claims in a poem that they came to Ireland riding in "flying ships" surrounded by "dark clouds." They landed on Sliabh an Iarainn (the Iron Mountain) in Co. Leitrim, where they "brought a darkness over the sun lasting three days." There is a lovely line which illustrates perfectly the bewilderment felt towards these conquerors;

"The truth is not known, beneath the sky of stars, Whether they were of heaven or earth."

A later version of the story relegates the flying ships to mere sailing ships. The dark clouds became towering columns of smoke as the ships were set alight, a warning to observers that the Danann were here to stay. Clearly, the monks recording this story were trying to make sense of something astonishing. [10]

Finally, it would not be possible to leave a discussion about whether or not the Fae are a seed race without paying a fair tribute to Andrew Power, the author of *Ireland, Land of the Pharaohs*. Power believed that the story of Noah's Ark was, in fact, the story of how our DNA...2 by 2...arrived on this planet. In this amazing work, which analysed a battle that took place much later, Power accidentally uncovered evidence of a lost race. "Decoding the raison d'être of the previously mentioned 'battle' uncovers the legend of a 'lost' race that has been, for the most part, erased from our conscious memory."[11] This battle, The Battle of the Boyne, took place in the 17th century. It was not a battle at all but rather a ritual re-enactment of what Power terms an Egyptian battle. My suspicion is that the primal battle upon which the Egyptian battle was based then will turn out to be a magical battle held millennia ago: The Battle of Moytura.

Throughout this work, we hope to show with clarity and precision just how obvious is the open secret; just how visible the traces of our ancestors for those with eyes to see and ears to hear. Those who became skilled in fracturing and fragmenting history have very nearly succeeded in their task. This eldest of the Celtic

---

[10] http://www.irishcentral.com/roots/ancestry/the-tuatha-de-danann-were-they-irish-gods-or-aliens-photos
[11] Power, J. *Ireland, Land of the Pharaohs*, p.2

tales describe a collision between two races: one from under the sea and one from a planet other than our own. The tale describes a blood sacrifice and a demand for blood that has never abated. We encounter the first 'human beings,' mixed offspring of these two races. We also follow a trail, a modern trail, like breadcrumbs through the forest of a fairy tale we know well; signs of our ancestors lives, legacy and culture, unmistakable clues we must protect and work to understand.

Chapter Two – The Mists

We have our Imagination as the translator between what is in the morphogenic field, which has been called pure potential, and the material plane in which we live. We are, in fact, magical creatures.

Rome never invaded Ireland but the Roman Catholic Church did. We can't even know when for sure but it is probably much later than we think, anytime between the first few centuries after the accepted date of Jesus' birth to 1550. Up until that time, until the time of the invasion of the entity known as Patrick, true descendants of the Fae would have been living complete lives together with the Druids. There may have been some invasion by the Vikings but considering the uncanny similarity between Norse myths and the earliest Irish tales, I really wonder if this is the same tale told again with a Norse flavour. There is archaeological evidence of ships and war garb and clothing and such that one assumes would match that of those belonging to Scandinavia. However, this book proposes that the Fae were the seed race, together with the Fomorans, and so the Vikings and all other peoples would have come from that line. In that case, naturally the tales would be quite similar. The tales from Iceland and Finland are very similar, as well. In fact, the Finns and the Frisians were quite likely immediate cousins of the Irish branch of the Fae and both figure quite prominently in what might be called a Middle History. Consider that. Middle History, in my view which accepts that history is patently false in its modern recounting and so the Catholic capture of Ireland was much later than we are told, would encompass most of the time between 10,000 BC or so to 0 AD. The newest datings of Egypt push us in that direction if nothing else! Datings from Egypt go much further back than that and my postulate is that the Fae predate the Egyptians[12]. Analysis of erosion of the Sphinx places Egypt at least at 10,000 BC. If the appearance of the first use of the swastika heralds the arrival of the Fae then we are looking at 40,000 BC. Of course, at the moment, this is conjecture.

Let us examine here the tales of the Tuatha de Danaan as they existed just after this time of the Battle of Moytura. Then we will track their immigration out over the world, as much as is possible, in terms of archaeological sites, language and etymology. There is also the moment of the appearance of the Sidhe, so beautifully discussed in this book by Maria Wheatley. If the Sidhe were/are according to some the result of a mingling of the Fae and humans then what are we actually talking about? Are we saying that the first mixture of Tuatha de Danaan and Fomoran…Lugh and Bres…are the first humans? I am making that claim. If then the Sidhe were a combination of those humans and the Tuatha de Danaan then the Sidhe would be yet another distinct race, more Fae than human. Bres and Lugh could have been considered progenitors of the Sidhe. Frankly we can all be considered to be Sidhe, in that

---

[12] http://www.jawest.net/

case. We must entertain the idea that these original Sidhe may well be these 'Survivors of Atlantis' referred to by Sylvie Ivanowa in her work. Andrew Power said he uncovered, as well, evidence of an extremely technologically advanced but ancient people in his work. Regardless, I personally think there is a distinct separation between the Fae and the Sidhe, an important one.

It is important to try to sort out as much as possible the time between the Battle of Moytura and the arrival of the church. An exhaustive treatment of that is beyond the scope of this book as we have many, many categories to tie together. However, it is such a key moment in redressing all the characters to suit the narrative of the church that we simply must account for it. In fact, I believe one of the later spinnings of the myth of the Tuatha de Danaan is a blatant admission of culpability by the church, revealed via very clever but potent Twilight Language.

It is a fact that the history of the Fae, then Tuatha de Danaan, was like everything else manipulated by the Jesuits completely after a certain point in time. Therefore, the histories which recount a defeat of the Tuatha de Danaan by the Milesians are extremely suspect. That the Milesians would have created a mist (cloak of concealment) already used by a Tuatha de Danaan man to meet a Fomoran woman and produce Lugh is far-fetched. It is also said the god of the oceans invented the mist to shield them from being seen after the Milesians banished them to the Underworld. I do not believe they were banished. I believe it was a choice they made, to wed themselves to the earth for some reason. It is in density that we find power. Remember, this was a people who wielded mighty magic, whether it was earth-derived, extra-terrestrial or both. Much of the history rewritten by the Jesuits was meant to justify the power of ruling families who were, in turn, set into place by the Vatican.

Here's what we need to know about the Vatican and the Catholic Church for the purposes of this discussion. Whatever the actual linear facts may be, it is the case that a God of the Seas is closely linked to the Vatican and the so-called Roman Catholic Christian Church, which has been demonstrated to be no more than a cult worshipping the Babylonian god Dagon.[13] The church can certainly boast that they banished the knowledge of our ancestors from our memories behind a veil or a mist, if you will, because the history we learn, for the most part, is manufactured. It is smoke and mirrors. As to the statement that the God of the Seas created a mist to hide the Thuatha de Danaan and then relegated them to the Underworld? That is a true statement of sorts. As to why the later tales would refer to this mist itself as the Faedh Fiadha is unknown. If it is some sort of joke, since Faidh is pronounced Faith, and the Catholic Faith was the mist drawn between us and the Fae then that is a reasonable explanation. The truth is the Cry of the Deer, or the Faidh Fiadha, was a spell or an invocation for protection if you will which was then appropriated by the church and renamed St. Patrick's breastplate or the Lorica. The stag or deer was associated

---

[13]http://www.kotipetripaavola.com/dagonfishgod.html

with the Head Druid, the Dagda. This incantation calls on all the earth's potency to stand between the utterer and the powers of evil. *It may also be that, in some way, whoever came with this Patrick entity was enough of a threat or required enough magic protection that the earth wedded the Fae to itself to protect them in response to the incantation.*

This does not alter the fact that the Fae already had the ability, the true and actual ability, to produce a mist and hide themselves. This is a theme throughout the tales. Even today, it is said that the Fae can make themselves visible whenever they choose to do so. However, this is another piece we need to sort out. The Fae have wedded themselves to the earth. The Sidhe, as their offspring and many humans are more than a little Sidhe in ancestry, are also said to hide in a mist and reveal themselves when desired. One of the most important tasks of this work is to untangle the knots. Who is who and what is what? And which of all of the above were The Survivors, those remnants of the long chase, those builders of the amazingly advanced communities that Sylvie Ivanowa says were populated by the same until just a few centuries ago?

It becomes clear that some serious research is necessary to try to piece together what the lives of the Fae would have been like, if we want to do so. It would be good to know what our basic gifts were and how they might have translated themselves over the ages. It would also be useful to piece some of that together and then stand what we think we know beside the megaliths and marvellous art and cities all over the planet. It seems reasonable to begin to uncover our true history rather than continue to live a lie. These marvels are OURS! Not some unknown entity unconnected to us. They belong to US. WE made them. Remember, too, that we will identify the predator by identifying who we are because the predator is who we are not. It is also a question as to when they actually did disappear behind the Faith. The Bardic Tales are the best place to look. Whatever is closest to the truth can be found there even if a bit of deciphering is necessary.

After the Battle of Moytura was over there would have been no more Fomorans. Why? Because the Morgue asked for every drop of blood from the battlefield. There are no remaining stories of giants with regard to Ireland as far as I can make out. It might be useful to hold in our thoughts this idea that the Fae, the victors and our ancestors, were Magic and that we have our Imagination...I Mage In, Magic.

My plan here is to try to suss out how these people lived but using resources which place the Bardic Tales as the end piece. I know that much can be gained from examining the etymological work of Landmann followed by some of the discoveries of Ivanowa. With those more modern sensibilities in place, the Bardic Tales may take on a new meaning.

Additionally, one could approach this problem based on the earthly standards which have been under such aggressive attack. That would be the air (and by extension, the sun), the seed, the soil, plant life especially trees, water, and resonance or frequency. Grant us that these are all methods or conduits through which or by which human beings communicate with or interact with our earth, whom I call Sophia. We could infer with a fair degree of safety that the Fae and their children up to a few hundred years ago were intimately involved with these categories. The Bardic Tales say so; the Faedh Fiadha leaves little doubt. The Fae were part of the natural world in the sense that there was a real communication, a real cause and effect going on. In fact, the very first clue I had personally that there was a massive esoteric component to the assault on us within the span of my lifetime was the clearly deliberate severing of us from direct contact with the sun through demonic changes in the plasma we call the atmosphere and the unprecedented and uncalled for dimming of the sun's output preventing such from reaching the surface of the earth.

Etymologically, we could separate the evidence into categories that would in some way imply a way of being in the world. We could add evidence, as least as far as Landmann demonstrated, of parts of the world. If we wanted to …or if you wanted to…rough dates could be established for enough of the etymological evidence to perhaps propose some sort of migration. Certainly, Landmann give us a rich etymological trail which describes their arrival from another planet:

"Let's look at the old feast of "Halloween", that is to mean, as can easily be seen, the "allo fairies", ("allo-feen") the "fairies from space", ('allo' : Ger., 'All=Space, Galaxy') from the universe. This festival, which was celebrated in early November was also known as "Sam Fiun" means "seed of the fairies". Note, the word "seeds of the fairies" refers to a sexual act of fecundity. Another name was "Samhain", ('Hain' an old German word for 'woods') the "seeds Hain" (the 'seed forest'). Christianity converted Halloween, from the feast of "Allfairies" to All Saints and All Souls Day. It is worth interjecting here that the festival of Halloween was forbidden in the USA by the Catholic Church as an obviously pagan festival and that it was associated by them as connected to Druidic blood sacrifices. It is what it is, a celebration commemorating the arrival of the Fae but, of course, the Pope does not want us to know that. At any rate, the Irish influx into the country because of the potato famine brought this festival to life in the United States. What is has become in that country is another matter altogether.

Linguistically this allo-feen idea finds wonderful proof in the fact that the English word 'Saint' equates to 'Sankt' in German, to mean 'to sink, to come down, to descend'. Thus the word "sanc ta" , 'to sink- descend- there' became later, after the confusion of tongues, converted to "holy" in it's allegedly Latin version. So the phrase, "All sanc ta" (which originally meant that the fairies from space came down from Planet Fee, also written Phe) "All sanc tus", was rendered in the alleged Latin termed feast of "All saints". The phrase "ce phe us" ("comes from the planet Phe") today also equated with designates a star constellation or the alleged Greek god of sleep "or phe us" ("from the planet Phe in the Urall") or the name of the old city "E phe sus" ("God of 'E' darted to the planet Phe") do offer such references to us. The Irish mythology is teeming with clues. There are the "Fe Arghus", the "arge (harsh) Fairy", whose spacecraft is the "Con Fearghus ". The "Con all" better of "Cun all" is the wedge-shaped (Allfahrzeug) space craft (Cun, Kun = wedge) and there is the phrase "Fe Arghus Fiodh Flio da" = the "arge" (harsh/bad/dark) Fairy flees to the (planet) Fe in the galaxy ODH ". Obviously the departure and return of fairies from space was always celebrated, and that not just on Halloween. The word "festival" attests to this fact. It reads: "Fee stib all", ("the fairy 'stibt' on into space," sputtering, "aufstiben" originally meaning "kicking, to fly up"). Likewise "fete" comes from fairies. The home of the fairies is "Avalon", is the "Au (watery plains) in space above". Spacecraft are called "vet, Phet", or "vehiculum, vehicle" in ancient texts.[14]

Having landed and lived on the island known as Eiru, and aside from the Bardic Tales we will consider in due course, we find linguistic evidence as we come closer to our own time. One of the ways they are mentioned in Ireland is as the Old People driven out by the Catholic Church. They were also known as Mannanon, or ancestors of men. I have also read reports of them in which they are referred to as the High People, the Gentle Folk, and the Noble Folk. As to making their way from Ireland, one would assume that these

---

[14]Landmann, E. The Women of the Planet Fe.
https://vortexcourage.me/2016/03/05/the-women-of-the-planet-fe/

would be the descendants of the Fae, whatever we want to call them now. In terms of identity, these travellers remained distinctly Fae for a very, very long time…long enough to leave an etymological roadmap.

For example, an immediate immigration strictly based on geographical proximity would be Wales and Scotland. It comes very much to mind that one crosses the Irish Sea by means of a *Ferry*. In Scotland, the Fae end up being associated with the Picts. In Wales, these beings were the Mamau or the Mamas. There are place names then in Germany, the Netherlands, and Switzerland which hint strongly that the Fae arrived there, too. Feyenoord in the Netherlands, Sass-Fee in Switzerland, and Fehndoorf, Veynau, Satzvery, Burgvey and Urfey in Germany. This list is the merest sampling of the place names globally that derive from some inhabitation by the Fae.

One really yearns, though, to have a better visual understanding of the Fae and their lives through the ages and hopes that such can be ascertained somewhat by the associated language. One hopes that an imagine of Walt Disney's Tinkerbell has not appeared in the reader's mind unbidden. We note, for example, that the Fae become very strongly identified and associated with the apparitions mentioned in so many cultures of women. They are known as the *Dames Blanches* in French, the *Damas Blancas* in Spanish, the Women in White in English. In Germany, they became the *Feen*, meaning fair, white and blonde. In Hungary, a bit of elevation was added or recognized in the name *Feher*, meaning noble Fee. This addition comes from the Old German *her* meaning sublime, holy or noble. That's interesting even just as a modern pronoun.

They are also characterized as magical no matter where they appear. For example, in Spanish and in Portuguese, they are known as *feticieros* (male) and *feticieras* (female). These words mean sorcerer. Indeed, they seem also always associated with a wand of some sort whether it is wooden or even made of metal and harnessing electrical impulses. (Although knowing what I know now about the true nature of movement on this planet, I would make a correction there and state that the wands channelled *magnetic* power). Again, we speak of movement, to move, as to ferry someone or something. Therefore, it makes sense that the migration is a big part of who they are or who they became. In light of Ivanowa's work, though, we have to ask, were they moving or being hunted? Use of language is a way of communicating known as 'Twilight Language,' which we will go back to later.

In the Ora-Linda-book it is reported that women (in Frisian "femna", in English "feme" = young woman, in French "femme") ruled the state. In this capacity they came to be known as Burgmagden (maids of the castle). City names such as Magdeburg or Magdala (near Weimar in Germany) testify to the Magdala fairy-Fe connection (Magdala = the "handmaid of the All", 'Universe'). The Bible carries many mentions of Magdalena ("magd – all – ena." – The maid beyond in space ") and religious scholars found that this does not necessarily denote the woman, who was placed as an acquaintance of Jesus in the drama of the New Testament. Hartmann von der Aue writes of the sorceress "Feimurgan", which broken down into a sentence suggests, the "Fei in Urgan", the fairy goes to Ur (all-space). Not to forget the festival Samhain, which some scholars of mythology translate it as "Ancestors Night", or the "Night of the Ancestors", as another example of revealing a deeper meaning when reading the words in their older context.

Looking at the evidence one can cull about the daily life of these ancestors from Sylvie Ivanowa's work, what she and her team uncover regularly are sites of technologically advanced but ancient cities either just under an identified culture or mis-identified as that culture. She points out, as do I and others, that often the symbol found in these areas common to all these sites globally is the swastika. For me, this is the calling card of the Fae. Ivanowa's work is absolutely critical in throwing off the veil over these magnificent forefathers. The application of Ivanowa's ideas to this work follows the path: there is ample evidence that very sophisticated cultures thrived globally millennia before the accepted historical version. She also presents an enormous amount of evidence that the cultures involved were so very able and understood how to use the earth's own magic to build and live as to be extraordinary, even magical. Ivanowa also presents a mountain of evidence that these sites, sites which could reveal our true history, are being covered over and destroyed regularly. Finally, she demonstrates that these sorts of archaeological and cultural sites were in full swing up until just a few centuries ago. It is my theory that the Fae were the driving force behind these sites up to a point and then their offspring continued to build and thrive globally.

Before we begin to have a look at these sites, we really have to discuss, as well, the idea that the timeline we have been taught is blatantly false. The dates have been changed from 900 AD onward, at least. The dates of older sites are genuinely upheld or pushed back even farther! This is where our Russian mathematician comes into the discovery story. The reason this is important to understand at this juncture is that much of the revised history was inserted to uphold the supremacy of the Roman Empire and likely then the Holy Roman Empire subsequent to that. As I have said, history has been seriously tampered with in order to justify modern power structures. Because this is so obviously the case, great pains have been taken to eliminate any real evidence (overwhelming evidence, at that) in extremely advanced and much earlier cultures.[15] Therefore, it is a real boon that we can combine the archaeological work of Ivanowa with the mathematical and statistical work of Fomenko in both casting extreme doubt on the popular notions of Rome and providing concrete evidence of other much greater, much older societies. It is here we will find evidence of our forefathers. Once we can discount the illusion we are all labouring under that has us believe that the Roman civilization was the inventor of all city planning systems, for example, we can entertain the reality that there were much older

---

[15]Fomenko, A. *History: Fiction or Science?*

cultures which were far more advanced. What I would like to do is present here some of Ivanowa's most compelling evidence regarding truly ancient cultures. Then I will visit in some depth the deconstructing of Rome by Anatoly Fomenko.

As Ivanowa says, we are told that we, now, are the high-tech crown jewel of civilization but are we? It's not even clear what materials constitute high-tech. In fact, it is more the methods of erection and the end result including use of or complementary accompaniment with what is already in place that marks an advanced civilization. All else is simply revenue generating for modern pyramid schemes and consortiums. When one observes a rock formation, for example, that turns out to be a building or dwelling it is of far more consequence that the corner are cut to laser-like precision, that the pieces fit seamlessly together with no nails or joints, that the dwellings have stood the test of eons. Our modern buildings are clunky, expensive, and unnatural and built for obsolescence. How better to sell you more buildings, my dear? There is always discussion regarding whether the stone is even cast from a geopolymer since the cuts are so excruciatingly, impossibly accurate. Our definition of high-tech must be re-evaluated. Our expectations must cease to be directed by glossy magazine ads. As Ivanowa asks, 'Are we just told these structures of ours are the highest of high tech so that we voluntarily confine ourselves to those prison cells?'

Ivanowa has found that the oldest documented dwellings lie underground. Is it possible then that the Fae being driven underground is both a metaphor *and* a reality? She has recently been investigating a type of construction referred to as Elf Castles. They can be found all over the world. If traditional dating methods are used just as a very general reference; these might be millions of years old. [16] The stones used are absolutely huge, they are set atop hills, and there seem to be no roads leading to and from. This only implies that perhaps other modes of transportation were used. These 'castles' are not stand alone as one might think when one imagines a British castle or German castle. There are generally half a dozen of these in an area forming a community. It is important to note, as well, that today we could never replicate what is already in place even with our 'high technology.' The advent of 3D printers may change that but in most cases, the 3D printers would have to be enormous. These things are not made by the peoples and tools supposedly in operation at the dates of these structures. How do we take seriously the line that these structures were shaped by people using stone tools softer than the stone they were shaping? Where does that lead us? Either it says the structures were made much, much earlier than reported and inhabited later by much less developed cultures or it says that these cultures were far more developed than we are allowed to know.

---

[16] https://www.youtube.com/watch?v=pGuBMcXEwzI

Additionally, she and many other researchers are investigating a multitude of underground tunnel 'cities,' globally. One of these was recently unearthed in the Caucasus in Russia. It is a very new discovery and has been named after the region, the Kabardino-Balkaria Megalith. It is as grand and as well constructed as the Great Pyramid of Giza. No attempt to date the location has yet been made. It is situated inside a man-made hill surrounded by natural hills. These are sized on the order of mountains, really. The people in the area say, this was so long ago that even we don't remember and we have been here thousands of years. The size of the city as it has been uncovered thus far, the quality of masonry and size of the stones, is all quite similar to Giza.[17] See visuals of Balkaria, which may have been a power plant attached to a technologically advanced city, below.

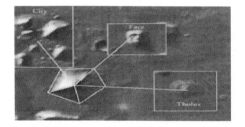

---

[17] http://survincity.com/2012/07/megalithic-cave-in-kabardino-balkaria/

Many ancient cites have within their confines inscriptions which speak of the magical beings who lived there. Three phenomena need our attention now, according to Ivanowa. Over-engineered shafts in megalithic tunnels that are all over the world and of uniform design; numerous interesting sites that have been selectively covered with mud or some other substance that could not have ended up there in any natural way; the possible artificial origin or some or even all deserts on the planet. How many of these have to do with the Fae? At least the first two. Balkaria is a great example of an over-engineered site.

Ivanowa notes that her studies of the underground cities, some of which are below other sites, indicate the same civilization built them all, and one capable of global travel, at that. She suggests that the Book of Velas is likely the most reliable source in terms of dates of antiquity as even the Vedas were written down relatively recently when the memory of human beings started to slumber, mostly disused. The huge fire-breathing dragon that is the human memory still lives. It simply has to be exercised and we have to unplug from the computer and the television until it is fully formed at roughly age twelve. (As a sidebar, I'd like to note that children are coming into the incarnation with perception issues that force them to rely on their memories rather than the written word. I do not think this is an accident.)

Before we continue discussing various types of extremely old cultural sites, it would be good to talk about Rome. The gold standards in marking advances in life altogether in our history, at least in the west, are in comparison with Greece and Rome. When it comes to modern life, we are constantly steered back to Rome as the seed of justice, law, architecture, city planning, oration, politics…the list is endless. This is why Dr. Anatoly Fomenko used Rome as a demonstration culture to show just how false and misleading our timeline actually is. The point then of bringing Rome into the discussion right now is this: the timeline was falsified by order of Pope Gregory for several reasons not the least of which is to bury the memory of any culture that came before. Why? Combined with the relentless determination to overlay the Catholic Christian religion on every soul on the planet it was meant to establish the infallible rulership of the Pope over all of the world as the only representative of Jesus. That is a very tall order, indeed. To succeed, in order to appear to be the final word on absolutely everything, there must be no contenders to the 'throne.' Best practice for this kind of avaricious totalitarianism is to wipe everything else out of the collective memory that has a chance of getting in the way. That certainly would put our ancestors the Fae and their issue, the Sidhe, squarely in their way. Especially important to remember, is that the Catholic Church is a prime purveyor of black magic. The Fae inheritance would bequeath to us full knowledge and ability to use our own magic and to see through the other.

Precursors to the magnificence that was "Rome" are plenty. Most of the world no longer knows that the technology in evidence at most of those sites is as good or better than the technology we credit the Romans for inventing. If our heads are pushed down into the textbook that says Rome is All every time we look up and see what else there may be, eventually we come to think Rome was all. In fact, the chronology or timeline we live by was written to make sure that happened. The monks who worked on the revision actually wrote themselves that they were not making exact copies but they were copying *and correcting.* This is why the official history does not fit with the artifacts and sites we have left. Then the history was imposed by military power underscored by the extreme cruelty of the Inquisition.

Let's mull this one over just a little bit. Who invented absolutely everything? Well, we all know the answer to that question, don't we? The Romans, right? Let's just have a look at one aspect for which Rome is celebrated: architecture and city planning. First of all, academics agree that the architecture of Rome was basically a simplification of the Greek style. Copying, folks, is not the same thing as inventing. There is an absolute abundance of sophisticated architecture that predates ancient Greece itself! Again, academicians say that ancient Greece arose on the ashes of Mycenae. At Mycenaean sites are found full-fledged water supply and sewage systems with running hot water on upper floors of buildings. Ancient aqueducts that have absolutely nothing to do with Rome are found in France.

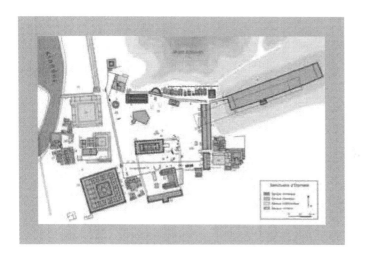

Peloponnese, Greece Dates In Question

Historians also classify Mycenae as a bronze age culture. If that is true, explain the machine tool marks in the structures of their unearthed cities. Bronze-age tools simply cannot do that kind of work. The stones used were exact replicas of those used in Peru and Egypt. However, experts note that even the Mycenae demonstrated a degradation of skills compared to older structures and so likely they did not invent much of this either. It is simply that we find these "Roman" inventions here and all over. Dozens, if not hundreds, of precision made aqueducts are found all over the world, even in the Americas and Mexico. The aqueducts actually feed 'pre-Columbian' cities such as were inhabited by the Aztecs. Large ruins of very similar styled building are found submerged near Cuba and in European waters.

I could go on for a very long time like this. However, my entire purpose is to demonstrate that there were so many advanced peoples living prior to Rome and to any other civilization which we are not allowed to venerate properly in this time. That coupled with the clear evidence for the Fae…these are the thrusts of my discussion. The question remains at this juncture: why would there be such an on-going and deep effort to hide all of this? Why is it we are meant to see ROME as the pinnacle of all? And, finally, who would benefit from that? Well, who ordered the history books to be rewritten? That's correct, a Pope in Rome. What devouring entity bent its maniacal will toward erasing any and all vestiges of 'pagan' cultures? Now there seems to be an actual 'machine' whose purpose is not just misinforming people about their actual heritage but organizing theft and destruction of sites and artifacts.

For example, in the Ukraine very deep in a mine was found the imprint or remains of what looks like an airplane wheel. This layer level should have been, according to modern dating, approximately 300 million years old. The day after the discovery, the mine was closed and the mine was filled with rocks and boulders. The photographic evidence we have comes from a worker with a cell phone. In the case of the Native American, most of the cultural evidence is boxed up and hidden away until lost from memory. Degradation in precision, materials and ability at the same sites speak to a loss of knowledge and connection (memory). ***However, some of the sites are not very old. It should be possible to trace the later path of these survivors based on the age of the sites, perhaps even to the final few.*** Star Forts are a fairly recent phenomenon yet there are some one finds under enough natural debris to indicate a sudden disaster of some sort. Additionally there are many *neo-classical sites*, even in the Americas, buried several stories underground.

Sylvie Ivanowa includes in her work some of her reading from a book called Seth Speaks by Jane Roberts. I include it because I, myself, am still looking for clues as to the arrival of a predator or parasite. I wonder if Seth is really speaking about the Survivors here, the descendants of the Fae? Perhaps this is a description of something else altogether, some sort of infection? He also speaks of the living voice that protested. I think that is important.

There came a time when some of the beings on this planet began to see the earth and everything on it as an object – to be taken apart and examined – rather than observed. But one must kill a thing to take it apart. You do not dissect something if you love it. When man began to dissect the universe on those terms he had already lost his sense of love for it. Only then could he examine it without being aware of the living voice that protested. When he then became cut off from nature he became cut off from conscious use of his abilities. [18]

On the other hand, philosopher Owen Barfield in a book called *Saving the Appearances, A Study of Idolatry*[19] discussed the transition of humanity from completely blended with the world around us to needing to completely sever ourselves from that and become sovereign. Now the idea is to be both of those things. These are concepts for the offspring of the Fae, not the Fae themselves. It is important to have a survey of the changes in how the world was viewed but it is also important not to assign these strategies or changes necessarily even to humanity. We are always on the watch for signs of our predator(s) or parasite(s). To me, this abrupt change in application of our skills would signal such. This bears watching as we continue to discuss the Tale of Humanity. *Seth Speaks* is a book I read in my early 20s, and cannot speak to anymore one way or the other, and the excerpt comes from the newearth series, not myself.

In summation, there is more than ample evidence that an extremely advanced civilization inhabited this planet and flourished until very recently. There is also ample evidence that the Catholic

---

[18] Roberts, J. Seth Speaks: The Eternal Validity of the Soul
[19] Barfield, O. Saving the Appearances, A Study of Idolatry

Church has bent its will to eliminating any memory of that civilization and supplanting itself as the highest of the high on the earth for all its inhabitants. This was accomplished by rewriting combined with destroying sites and artifacts. These projects are on-going.

Chapter Three - *Kreisen*

We have our Imagination as the translator between what is in the morphogenic field, which has been called pure potential, and the material plane in which we live. We are, in fact, magical creatures.

Ley Lines, Trees, Water, Frequency, and Sun. From beyond antiquity, these shepherds of the strength of Sophia, the Fae would be pulled more and more into a conscious arena by the demonic attacks on these *Kreisen*. This word in German is used for childbirth. It is the circle or going in a circle, circulation. All these things have deeply to do with the circulation of Sophia. The water, the breath of the trees which appear as capillaries in lungs, and the ley lines which are carriers not of electrical energy but magnetic energy. It is magnetic energy which levitates. Anything that rises or swims is actually levitating via vortexes according to Viktor Schauberger. A bird does not fly, for example, it is 'being flown.'[20] A fish does not swim, it is 'being swum.' A tree grows by levitation. These energies are the true, fundamental energies of our world. (Rudolf Steiner wrote that electricity is actually biological debris in a way, detritus and death.)

---

[20]Alexandersson, O. *Living Water, Viktor Schauberger and the Secrets of Natural Energy.*

The ley lines' magnetic veins within the earth along with water are half the blood-respiratory system of a living being. The other half is the sun. The sun sends. The earth receives. And vice versa. When all is gathered together, thrumming and humming properly, there is a frequency. The earth emits a frequency. All the life on the planet, including us, resonates to this frequency. We, in turn, generate our own frequency and all frequencies resonate to each other. This is true, authentic communication. Most communication happens on a non-verbal level. Our words are used to create, to pull from the morphogenic field, translate through our imaginations, and produce or materialise here on this plane. Our vocal chords produce frequency when they vibrate.

The ancient texts tell us the most important part of any ancient technology and that is the use of sound. In the Vedic scriptures, we read how sound was used by the original engineers of the universe. The frequency in sound can shift matter around by virtue of vibration.

The plasma we humans swim in, that which lies between us and our sun, has become something to change physically and chemically to block as much of what comes from the sun as possible. The ley lines have been severely disrupted. For millennia, those who would harness or funnel earth energy in some way located and tapped into the ley line energy or the water energy. The earth was informed by the sun and by water. Now this energy is being destroyed. Yes, one wonders why and by whom. Clearly, this is being done by some entity who does not need natural energies or who simply has a short-term interest in destroying the living being of the planet. However, it is also possible that the perpetrator has need of an instrument retuned. If we think of our living planet as an instrument, a resonator of sound, then the general idea of re-tuning her for some purpose may be a reasonable one. These vicious aberrations, created despite the protest of the planet itself, may support a form of life quite unlike ourselves. Additionally, we have stated that there is a parasitic nature to our predator. It feeds off negative emotions, fear, and the adrenalized terror that goes along with bloodshed. It may simply be tuning the earth to that sort of pitched stress in order to feed off her, as well. This sort of scenario would bring the Fae forward and that is the point.

When I began on my own to investigate the idea of the association of the Fae with the ley lines, I was truly dismayed to find a body of work dismissing the existence of such a connection but rather talking about the 'ghost roads' and the fairies who guard them. These would be the travelling paths of the deceased. The ley lines, of course, are a well-documented power grid and the Fae are well connected with these grids. The initial statement is like a nightmare visit from Walt Disney. What might be hiding behind such a characterization is either the idea that human energy goes into the ley lines post corporeal existence OR it may be an authentic reference to the withdrawal of the Fae into the earth's energies. However, I am also learning about Shadow Language, what you and I might call allegory or metaphor but with a real kick. It is something many understand intuitively and I did not know it had a name. The understanding of Shadow Language would be one of the gates keeping people unready for knowledge squarely on their own tracks. However, the time is now for everyone to understand who we are. There can be no more Secret Club. All the secrets are open secrets anyway just sitting there waiting to be seen and understood. So, let's push it.

Friend and co-author, Maria Wheatley has assured me that this attitude about the Fae and the ghost paths is an extremely recent (perhaps twenty years?) development and little regarded. As the Fae and their offspring (human beings) appeared and evolved they used certain numerical formulas over and over again in nature and in certain places (usually marked by a specific kind of name) to amplify a kind of unique energy, or *magnetism*. Certainly these forces were collected up, I believe, much like a modern audio system would be able to condense and amplify and direct such energy. Later, I think, it was at these spots that they built the first temples, measured to the exact specifics of the sacred geometry they had observed in nature or, even more likely, that they had been taught. From there it was determined the optimum time to perform magick rituals, on numerically significant dates and magnetically significant locations. I think it is really interesting that we refer to this as a magick ritual and not a natural expression of our ability. This magnetic energy occurred along paths or tracks that ran across the Earth and overlapping at various crossroads, which were the preferred locations of holy centres. In modern times, this is recognized again and designated as ley lines. There were many phenomena that appeared or were noticed at the sites of ley line energy such as place names or even surnames of local families but ley was selected and used.

Back in what have been called the 'Middle Ages,' the location of which in space and time is entirely unknown and even in question as having ever existed, the Vatican ordered that its churches be constructed on the sites of old temples whenever possible. The tradition of sacred places runs deep and seems to be largely based upon the continuous observations of paranormal manifestations. The entities who allegedly approached human beings in miraculous events frequently ordered a church or temple built on that spot. The miraculous occurrences could have simply been appearances of the Fae, however I truly doubt that the Fae would have instructed a real interference with their energy source. This would have been a manifestation of the Predator or even what we might call the Bad Fairies. The Fae would not have needed a church spire to harnass and direct the manifesting abilities of a ley line site. These tools have appeared constructed by entities who had either lost the wisdom or never had it in the first place. At this point, we see the beginnings of unenlived creative attempts. These sites would be landmarks for the enemy, the jealous ones.

Wanting to present a very real description of the current damage to ley lines, I interviewed Maria Wheatley, who is an expert in this field. Here are the questions and answers:

In what way are the leylines being deeply damaged right now?

Ever since roads crossed leys and more importantly the dragon lines-earth currents were cut through which
the Chinese called amputated, the energy system has been affected.
The building of roads have cut the Dragon Lines. Clearly you have groups that project their will into the system and abused it. Himmler set all the concentration camps on the red and white energy currents and this is where they got the colour of the Nazi flag from. Feed into the lines pain and fear and they can reflect it especially if large scale sacrifices occurred in the camps. MW

There was so much bloodshed both during and after that war. First those gathered up by the Nazis such as Jews, gypsies, gays and so forth and then the Germans gathered after the war who also died in the camps. One can hardly conceive why even more blood was necessary after the horrors of the part of the Great Battle known as World War II. Prisons and orphanages and such have been located in great numbers along leylines.

Placing 'power objects' on these currents after a sacrifice holds the energy like an anchor - Himmler did this, so many say, I was asked to find something along these lines but was guided not to. Sound also acts as an anchor, especially if there are standing stones on the line. Removal of standing stones can weaken the overall energy network. Tall buildings jar and 'stab' global grid lines. New World Order used negative global grid systems for the placement of prisons and orphanages - some global grids enhance and induce fear

and paranoia   MW

Of course, that makes me wonder if very powerful ley line grids exist under cities with lots of skyscrapers. This would be a way of harnessing and using that energy for other reasons or perhaps just drawing the power away from the earth to weaken her in some way. But even before that came the placement of radio towers atop sacred mountain sites, such as the mountain just outside Frankfurt where Siegfried 'woke' Brynhilde, and the ordering of all broadcasts of any kind and all recordings of any type to be made at a frequency significantly higher than the earth's natural frequency.

CERN in Geneva sits on important ley lines and crossings. How is CERN affecting those lines?

CERN is close to a number of lines. Here is a ley network discovered in 1920s by Xavier Guichard of France, its focus is on and emerges from Alaise in South France close to border (between France and Switzerland). CERN as a circle - the circle in itself generates Form Energy - a series of concentric circles of power within and without of the circle. Even a circle drawn on a bit of paper will do this. It can be protective as in salt occult circle and aids manifestation.

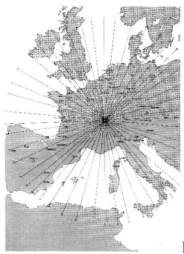

Imagine, if you will, this
amazing array of ley lines which do emanate from one spot in
France, with the overlay of latitude lines we know are there. Latitude
lines may be an artificial construct or they may simply be us
applying what we know unconsciously. Then imagine, if you will,
that you are a Fae or a Druid and you are standing at the very centre
of the ley lines. They fan out around you. You begin to sing or
vocalize or in some other way produce a clear, pure sound. This
affects the vortexes in the air in which we live and in terms of
frequency the centre point begins to rise. We cannot see it with our
eyes likely but it lifts and it forms a Hyperbolic Tower of Sound,
also known as a Pythagorean tower.

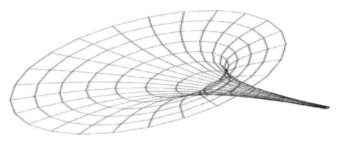

What sort of frequency/resonance power point would that become? Set the image above the map on its head so that the bell sits on the ground. What could be manifested with such a thing? Why is CERN so tantalizingly close to such a power area? And, more important than any of this, why did CERN put out a call recently for artists and creative people to come on board? The Imagination, folks. The power grid, the sound bell and the Imagination. What cannot enliven and manifest still seeks to piece it together in a kind of Frankenstein fashion. This dastardly scenario would alert the keepers of the earth to come forward. I doubt the artists have any idea how they are really being used.[21] This is NOT the Fae nor the Fae's descendants. It is the Predator. That which cannot enliven and manifest still seeks to piece it together life or an imagination made from sticks and rubber bands in a kind of Frankenstein fashion.

There is such a thing as a song line in Australian aboriginal culture. Are song lines ley lines walking? There are many different methods of pre-literate navigation that have been documented

[21] http://arts.cern/collide

around the ancient world. The Aboriginal fusion of navigation and oral mythological storytelling is likely to have been a common method in the past and goes a long way toward explaining the development of sacred landscapes.

Song-lines, also called Dreaming Tracks, are paths across the land (or sometimes the sky) which mark the route followed by localised 'creator-beings' during the Dreaming. The paths of the Song-lines are recorded in traditional songs, stories, dance, and painting. By singing the songs in the appropriate sequence, Indigenous people could navigate vast distances, often travelling through the deserts of Australia's interior. The continent of Australia contains an extensive system of song lines, some of which are of a few kilometres, while others traverse hundreds of kilometres through lands of many different Indigenous peoples.

A knowledgeable person may navigate across the land by repeating the words of the song, which describe the location of landmarks, waterholes, and other natural phenomena. In some cases, the paths of the creator-beings are said to be evident from their marks, or petroglyphs, on the land, such as large depressions in the land which are said to be their footprints.

Since a Song-line can span the lands of several different language groups, different parts of the song are said to be in those different languages. Languages are not a barrier because the melodic contour of the song describes the nature of the land over which the song passes. The rhythm is what is crucial to understanding the song. Listening to the song of the land is the same as walking the Song-line and observing the land. In some cases, a song-line has a particular instruction, and walking the wrong way along a song-line may be a sacrilegious act (e.g. climbing up Uluru where the correct direction is down). Traditional Aboriginal people regard the land as sacred, and the songs must be continually sung to keep the land "alive". This is the same in many indigenous cultures, particularly the Native American populations come to mind. They sang to the earth constantly and therefore had to be silenced. They also drummed to the earth and so had to be silenced.

The ley lines are about magnetic frequency. The Fae are the guardians of the same. The Aborigines of Australia emit frequency in the very magical, very human resonance of vocalizations...songs in this case....and become living, walking ley lines in a way.

Before I leave this subject to my esteemed colleague, Maria Wheatley, I would like to add just a few pieces of information. Ley lines are global. They do not just run through Britain and Europe. For example, "In several other parts of the world, lines linking holy centres are not only mythological paths down which the gods representing the various heavenly bodies pass at regular seasons, but have some further quality known only to native magicians. American Indians, particularly the Hopi of the American Southwest, appear to use them as *cables of communication*. The Australian Aboriginals use them as road maps. Perhaps, even their custom of Walkabout for their adolescents is a finding of and tuning into or even being recognized and accepted by the ley energy beneath them.

In China, they are known as *lung-mei*, the paths of the dragon, and run between astronomical mounds and high mountains. The Chinese believe that *lung-mei* extended all over the world, and this belief is everywhere supported by evidence of local tradition.

In Ireland, "these paths, sometimes visible as old road (were said to be used by) fairies who passed through the land, and everyone who stood in their way might be struck dead or taken off and never seen again."[22]

Eventually, once the Catholic Church began its devouring operation, orders were passed down to erect a church atop every power centre. The sacred sites for the most part would have been well-known and used. The practice of locating the terrestrial magnetic current was not confined to prehistoric times. Every Christian church was similarly sited. When we discuss the sites being impaled by skyscrapers and a church atop each power centre, I can't help but think of Manhattan with its towers everywhere and its sister borough across the river, Brooklyn, also known as the City of Churches. The United Nations is located there in the centre of all that, as well, a tower itself stretching upward.

Being surrounded by water or on the sea board amplifies the power of a region immensely. Water is Memory and

---

[22]Michell, J. *The New View Over Atlantis.*

Communication: 4 to 60 water molecules form a 'cluster'. Each cluster stores about 440k bits of data or information so what happens to information transfer or conversation between anything on the surface of Sophia or beyond and the actual entity of Sophia. Additionally, as we 'carry' water within us clearly this is a primary way we communicate with the entirety of the world. Each other, all life on it and the planet itself, the atmosphere and so on.[23] This is very much a component of fracking and of so-called geo-engineering. What happens to a part of the earth and its people when no rain falls? What happens when a river is diverted? And, as Ivanowa says as an extreme example, what about areas of the planet that may have been made desert artificially? What kind of natural com- munication occurs for those areas? Are they completely cut off? Why?

Dr. Masaru Emoto was the most prominent and well-known modern researcher to get this idea that water carries information to the public...or back to the public. Even if not mandated to protect the water systems (Guardians of Blood, so to speak), any earth shepherd would note with some genuine alarm that the communication systems seemed to be down thanks to what's happening with the planet's water. The work of Emoto, Viktor Schauberger and now Carly Newday, is paramount in understanding how sentient life on this planet actually does communicate. We tend, I believe, to use our larynx and vocalizations to create. We communicate in a myriad of ways. Yes, the Fae are the Guardians of the Ley Lines. However,

---

23Newday, Dr. C *Water Codes*

my suspicion now is that they are organically part of the magnetic energy of this planet and so that places them everywhere there is energy, everywhere there is communication, and everywhere there is creation. Regardless, the water in the earth and our bodies is where memory lives and if wiping out a particular memory is the goal then water is a target!

If water carries IN-FORMation then everything that takes in and uses water is in-formed by it. If it is alive, it is in-formed by water. But that's not the end of it by any means. Viktor Schauberger's work strongly indicates that it is, in fact, the vortexing properties around us that allow for movement, energy conveyance and growth. In researching the Fae we find that: there is a rather long-standing belief that they are inextricably linked to the ley lines, the earth's magnetic energy lines; mythology ties the Fae strongly to the trees, as well, which are the most organized of the plant life connected to air and to respiration. Living water itself is a form of communication pathway, absolutely essential to the stability of the planet and certainly to growth. All of these living pathways and communication organisms are forms of vortex/magnetic energy. It appears we are rapidly heading in this discussion toward the confirmation that the Fae are simply the Guardians of Magnetic Energy. Having said that, when one ponders the hyperbolic sound tower and the ley lines, with an eye toward manifestation and creation, then one can, I believe, imagine what the ancestors were like on this planet and why the tales of them seem so mighty and magical. One can also absolutely imagine how great cities were built without modern equipment which isn't up to the job anyway. It is also, I believe, important to note that all of these capacities and tools lie here still, perhaps a bit dormant, waiting for rightful use. It is also important to begin to view on an everyday level the human voice as a magnetic force or magnetic energy. And, we have simply got to wake up to the powers and forces which are destroying all of this as fast as we wake up. It is a race.

The opposition seems better at using and promoting electricity, which is a dead thing, the carcass of waste as Rudolf Steiner noted, and can be sold for profit. Meanwhile, entities such as CERN situate themselves very close to extremely powerful ley line sites and one can only assume not by accident. (That makes it even more amusing when a creature such as weasel gets into the works at CERN and wreaks havoc.) We are surrounded by our own magic all the time and yet we no longer see as the opposition has made it their goal to sever us from this. One of the best ways to do that is to relegate the idea of these ancestors to the fairy tale slush pile and mock any serious consideration of what came before as infantile or crazy. Stop believing it.

We can demonstrate that places of great magnetic power were conscripted. After the megalithic period, they were covered with temples of one sort or another and then, like an unstoppable steamroller, the Catholic Church erected their 'churches' atop energy sites, channelling power up and/or down through the spire. In the 20th century, however, we see the advent of a truly horrific frequency adjustment with the radio and television towers stabbed into the top of mountains and hills, many of which have been known as traditional sites of feminine energy such as the hill dedicated to Brynhild outside Frankfurt, Germany. In fact, the site was one Hildegrade of Bingen journeyed to. The radio tower built there is actually called Siegfried (male energy penetrating the top of the mountain). At CERN, we see a statue of Shiva outside their main building in Geneva. Inside, it is said that the name of the fine calibrating mechanism is called Kali, who is the consort of Shiva.

Heinrich Himmler understood the great power of the natural frequencies and, it seems, determined to kick them off natural, jar them enough to interrupt the natural communication between human and earth. Even music is recorded at a frequency higher than 'normal.' Since the inception of this program, which can only be seen as intensely damaging to people and the planet, many other artificial forms of frequency have appeared such as that coming from the GWEN towers and, as ever, the profoundly destructive nature of the microwave.

We have attempted to explain in what ways the Fae are attached to natural earth magnetic energies and to describe the demonic attack on such which has become so very intense in the 20th century. We have, we hope, answered any question as to why the Fae would return now and why. We don't really need to discuss for these purposes what's happened to the conductive properties of the human body or how the plasma around us (the air) has been damaged and changed. Suffice it to say that interfering with both the connection to the sun and, frankly, with our ability to see is what's happening. Schauberger indicated we need an atmosphere in order to see anything. Therefore, if we change the atmosphere, that cannot help but affect what we can see...the visual spectrum...for good or ill. Could it be that even when the Fae want us to 'see' them, we may not be able to?

Chapter Four - The Women

We have our Imagination as the translator between what is in the morphogenic field, which has been called pure potential, and the material plane in which we live. We are, in fact, magical creatures.

Inevitably, when one spends time with the Tuatha de Danaan, The Fae or the Sidhe, one realizes that there is an overarching and undeniable feminine gesture that has lived on through the ages. It really is as if a woman comes to take your hand and lead you through this terrain. The first time I encountered it myself was typical. I was contacted by a friend of a friend, called Jamie. We shared coffee and wonderful discussion about the as-yet-unknown to me incident of The Battle of Moytura. As the hours passed and we made ready to part company, he said to me that he wanted to tell me one last story. As a little boy in Ireland, his parents had taken him to the area around the Boyne River. Wandering on his own, he was met suddenly by the vision of a woman. It seemed they knew each other. Still the boy was amazed as a small boy would be. After a few minutes, the woman leaned over and whispered in his ear, "shhhh...we're not supposed to be here!" Then she vanished. Jamie looked at me and said, "That was you, Cara. I recognized you right away." There is always the woman in the story of the Fae.

In my research, I would pinpoint the first encounter of this sort to just prior to the second Battle of Moytura. This was the comely maiden, very beautiful and very young according to the Bardic Tales, who placed herself to waylay the Head Druid, the Dagda (pronounced Doy-da) as he went to join the bloodbath. She was the daughter of the mighty battle leader of the Fomorans herself and used what I would have called spell and counter-spell, really, in a magickal dual with the Head Druid to try to keep him away from the battle. Some versions of the story have her relinquishing and joining in, using the deadly art of the wand, and vanquishing one-ninth of the opposing army, her own father's army. Whether or not that was the case I believe should be considered with care. I have heard the tale told in Bardic fashion with no mention of the magic of the woman engaged in the bloodbath. The only woman related to that second battle of Moytura interested in blood was the Morgue. I have seen it in print with this as the ending. I will always side with the oral histories.

The intensely feminine gesture of the stories of the Tuatha de Danaan and hence the Fae and then even the Sidhe spring, I believe, from the tales of goddesses who, by and large were offspring of Aine, the original 'goddess' or the Dagda and one of the original females. They were Boann and some say her daughter, Brigid, just to name a few. In fact, Brigid is a threefold 'goddess', just as the Norse characters of the Norns who seemed to have inherited the Dagda's cauldron were. It is worth a study at some point to determine why these offspring or inheritors of the Druidic magic were threefold suddenly. It seems a bit of a degradation in some way. Of course, it is critical to remember that Brigid is the feminine aspect of the Fae stolen by the Catholic Church and reappointed, as with all other things, to its aims as the character of St. Brigid. Brigid's Day is, also critical to remember, 2 February. FE-bruary. She was stolen because she was simply so powerful they could not make her go away.

The physical appearance of the Tuatha de Danaan has been made not of here and there: physically outstanding, tall, red-haired, fair-skinned, aristocratic and mystical beings who mingled with the others but remained apart. Their principal residence was, supposedly, the Boyne Valley, with Tara as their capitol.[24]

It is easy enough to discuss what has so often been discussed, that being the fact of feminine deities throughout all of mythology, leading as we shall see once again to the Roman Catholic entity of Mary. In fact, we are so accustomed to such a discussion it is likely to put us to sleep and leave us unready for a moment of insight. What is more pertinent to our purposes in this book is to discuss the phenomenon of apparition. In every culture, there is the apparition of a female entity, whether as a maiden, as a hag, as a goddess or as Mary the mother of Jesus. We shall begin by simply mentioning a few of the Celtic goddesses. It is then very important that we spend time with Brigid followed by the Lady of the Lake and finally, apparitions and white ladies around the world. I often wonder why the oracles are left dangling on their own, as these are, in my mind, clearly Fae candidates. In the end, we simply must land on the co-

---

24Fitzpatrick, J. *Erinsaga*

opted phenomenon of visitations from Mary Mother of Jesus. Hopefully, we will be able to burrow down to what's under this and not fall into the easy regurgitation which leads nowhere.

After Danu, the goddess from whom all Tuatha de Danaan were said to have sprung, we come to Eriu and Aine. It can be quite difficult to find tales of any of these characters that reliably pre-date the Jesuit history grinder of the 16th century. My point is not necessarily to dwell on goddesses and their unearthly power anyway. My purpose is to dwell on their offspring, the Fae, and the set of capacities we all share. It is likely better to spend more time on Brigid than any other as she subdued the church rather than the church subduing her. Additionally she came to be known as the Woman in White. This description followed the female apparitions across the globe and down through the ages.

From Encyclopedia Mythica on Brigid: Name Cognates: Breo Saighead, Brid, Brighid [Eriu], Brigindo, Brigandu [Gaul], Brigan, Brigantia, Brigantis [Briton], Bride [Alba].

Breo Saighead, or the "Fiery Arrow or Power," is a Celtic three-fold goddess, the daughter of The Dagda, and the wife of Bres. Known by many names, Brighid's three aspects are (1) Fire of Inspiration as patroness of poetry, (2) Fire of the Hearth, as patroness of healing and fertility, and (3) Fire of the Forge, as patroness of smithcraft and martial arts. She is mother to the craftsmen. Sons of Tuireann: Creidhne, Luchtaine and Giobhniu. Excalibur, a sword clearly held by the Fae as one of the four implements of magick they always carried, was forged by the Lady of the Lake. That figure smply must be associated with Brigid due to her fire and forge aspect.

Brigid, which means "one who exaults herself," is Goddess of the Sacred Flame of Kildare (derived from "Cill Dara," which means "church of the oak") and often is considered to be the **White Maiden aspect of the Triple Goddess.** She was Christianized as the "foster-mother" of Jesus Christ, and called St. Brigit, the daughter of the Druid Dougal the Brown.

Brighid's festival is Imbolc, celebrated on or around February 1 when she ushers Spring to the land. During this time Brigid personifies a bride, virgin or maiden aspect and is the protectoress of women in childbirth. Imbolc also is known as Oimelc, Brigid, Candlemas.

Gailleach, or **White Lady,** drank from the ancient Well of Youth at dawn. In that instant, she was transformed into her Maiden aspect, the young goddess called Brigid. Wells were considered to be sacred because they arose from *oimbelc* (literally "in the belly"), or womb of Mother Earth. Because of her Fire of Inspiration and her connection to the apple and oak trees, Brighid often is considered the patroness of the Druids.

The Lady of the Lake: bestower of Sovereignty, weaver of magicks, maker of the magical sword Excalibur, healer of the wounded King -- what potent visions of an elder and enchanted time her legend brings to mind! And yet, if we go back to the original Arthurian material, composed in Wales during the 12th century and earlier, we do not find her. Nor was she a product of the later French Arthurian romances.

The Lady of the Lake is older still, older than Celtic Christianity; she is the Irish Goddess/Saint Brigid, the Welsh enchantress Ceridwen, and many other Ladies of the Depths -- the primal Dark Mother Goddess, patroness of Celtic Shamanism. Is Brigid all of them and are they each, a piece of Brigid? Brigid, then, would be the first power to capture and convert by the Catholic Church upon their landing in Ireland. Again, we must remember that Ireland was never conquered by the Roman Army but only by the Roman Catholic Church. This is a fascinating fact. My sense is that Brigid has been doing battle with the church for a very long time.

Since Brigid is the guardian of many wells in Britain and Ireland, we might expect her to answer, "Brigid", but instead she replies, "My name is Sovereignty." But remember, the Romans renamed Brigid after their own bestower of sovereignty, suggesting that while this aspect of Brigid may not have survived in direct form after Roman times, it was familiar enough during them.

Note also, that the sword of Arthur's sovereignty, Excalibur, came to him out of a lake. The Lady of the Lake is a shadow of the goddess Sovereignty, the mother of kings and heroes, and she is indeed both hideous ("evil") and beautiful ("good"), both a manipulative enchantress and a giver of good things, in true ambiguous Trickster fashion.

Another tricksterish tale surfaces in the "Life of St. Brigid":
she gets the land for her shrine and abbey from an avaricious bishop
by getting him to swear that she can have as much land as her cloak
will cover. Although he thinks he's got the best of the bargain, he
doesn't know Brigid is a goddess, whose lore tells that she hung her
cloak on the sun's rays to dry. When she threw out her cloak, it
spread in glittering billows for acres, and her sacred place was thus
preserved. Perhaps Brigid's most clever trick was to transform
herself from a goddess into a Christian saint, thus assuring that the
very Church opposing Irish paganism would perpetuate her tales and
lore.

It is important to stay with the apparition of the Lady of the
Lake. We have, I think, established the idea that water is one of the
sources of magnetic energy quite thoroughly guarded by and dwelled
in by the Fae. We have established that one of the four symbols of
power always with the Fae is the sword. Hence, if a woman rises
from a Lake and hands the sword of power, or blessing, to a would-
be king, this is to be seriously seen as communication between the
Fae and their offspring. In fact, twilight language leads us to
potentially believe that Lancelot du Lac was a child of the Lady of
the Lake and an unnamed male. Or there is the tale that he was
stolen as a baby and raised in her realm.

It is quite possible that the Lady of the Lake, as a likely
incarnation of Brigid, is a critical part of linking humanity to the
ancient aspect of the Fae. She is completely removed from the earth;

she dwells in the waters of Avalon. She is often confused with Nimue, as well as being mislabeled as Merlin's wife and seducer. The real Lady of the Lake is none of these. She is a supernatural being that maintains the link between fae and mankind because she keeps the magical weapon Excalibur, releasing it to whom SHE deems worthy. In this case, Arthur Pendragon, son of Uther. All of this, of course, is assuming that these characters and this tale was not rewritten to justify kingdoms, as was so often the case after 1550. There is, though, the very real fact that Welsh history books, as such, were confiscated and burned and replaced in the 1920s as they were replete with references to Arthur and Wales. Had these simply been fantasies, the books would have been left in place as no threat. So it seems some of the true history was saved.

The lady is a mysterious figure in Arthurian legend, and Merlin himself recognizes he is beneath her in 'rank' or dwelling. She is completely other- when Arthur goes to the lake, in some legends spurred by Merlin, he hesitates to take the sword, and Merlin tells him to do so. Yet, Merlin does not communicate with the lady or step forward to take the sword for him, presenting it to Arthur himself. In fact, Merlin's lineage has been drawn to the Fae.

She embodies the Fae association with water, such as she who guards the Boyne River- the goddess Boann. This is an easy thing when one considers water as a sentient being, interconnected and global, yet separate and local. She also reflects the best aspects of Brigid, daughter of the Dagda. Brigid is a protector of water and rivers, streams, and also tends the fire. However, Brigid and Boann are not the same thing. (Interestingly, at Kildare, the flame of Brigid was guarded by 19 virgins, dressed in Crimson and carrying swords. None spoke to men.) Brigid becomes key as she marks the transition between Celtic/Fae Ireland and Roman Catholic Ireland, in that the church stole her and her power and turned her into a Catholic saint.

The sword being delivered -or returned - to Arthur by the lady is significant in not only its presentation, but that it is 'blessed' both by water and earth (pulled from stone). This however, translates in some texts as an ANVIL (which is critical, considering the fae and their relationship to iron). The anvil is also critical in that we move from stone to anvil when we move from the Fae history to the Norse tales. I have seen what can only be called a replica of the sword in the stone at Galgano in Italy. It is somehow connected with a St. Galgano.

Upon Arthur's death, the sword is returned to the water, and the Lady of the Lake. As Arthur lay dying from a mortal wound, he asks sir Bedevere to return Excalibur to the water. When Bedivere betrays him twice, seeing the weapon should not be 'wasted', Arthur tells him he absolutely must return it, that his life-his soul- depends on it. When Bedevere does finally throw the sword into the water, the arm comes out of the water and retrieves the blade, shaking it three times, and returning beneath the water.

Considering that, one can note that our Lady is the link to the old land, the water, old ways, etc...she is a deity, Fae, in true possession of the weapon and chooses its carrier, therefore choosing the king and descendants of the throne. And when we relax and start to refer to this entity as Our Lady, we are transported unbidden and unwilling to a vision of the Catholic 'Our Lady', Mary. Indeed it is worth thinking about: is every church or grotto called Our Lady of Something-or-other truly a temple to Mary? Or is it Our Lady of the area?

Is it possible that the Oracles were simply remnants of the more powerful Fae? Again, the divining would happen via the medium of water. Sybil. Certainly Brigid was known for her ability to 'divine' the future. The three-fold Norns were able to determine past, present and future and assign destiny. So what about these characters known as the Oracles?

The research seems to indicate that there was likely a development within political, religious and social life in which claiming powers of prophesy bestowed great personal power to the claimant. In fact, it smacks of the unenlivened creation we speak of when trying to identify what is a human creation and what is not. Deep investigation into this statement is beyond the scope of this book however does merit more investigation by any researcher looking to differentiate between authentic, enlivened creation and parlour tricks meant to entice a population. These appearances, in my mind, are very likely to herald the appearance of the parasite on the planet.

Nevertheless, there are a multitude of spontaneous sightings of so-called Women in White all over the world and in every culture. Cultural references to these Fae apparitions include....as we can see many of these appearances occur in the same places year after year. Some refer to these entities as 'para-humans.' The Angels keep to their ancient places as written by the poet Francis Thompson.

Unfortunately sightings of so-called White Ladies, meaning one would suppose ladies dressed in white, have been summarily relegated to the ghost story genre. In fact, this tale is told many places around the world in which there exist legacies of potent feminine gestures in ancient cultures, the *Matre* image described in culturally relevant terms, echoing the original event in Ireland. A typical example is that of the *Mouros Encantados* of the Pyrenees region. Have a look at this entry in wikipedia and see if the twilight language becomes apparent: The **moura encantada** is a supernatural being from the fairy tales of Portuguese and Galician folklore. She often appears singing and combing her beautiful long hair, golden as gold or black as the night with a golden comb, and promises to give treasures to whom sets her free by breaking her spell. (In Galicia, though, they are more commonly **redheads.**) According to Jose Leite de Vasconcelos, *mouras encantadas* are "*beings compelled by an* *occult power to live on a certain state of siege as if they were numb or asleep, insofar as a particular circumstance does not break their spell"*. According to ancient lore, they are the souls of young maidens who were left guarding the treasures that the <u>*mouros encantados*</u> (enchanted mouros) hid before heading to the Mourama. The legends describe the mouras encantadas as young maidens of great beauty or as charming princesses who are "dangerously seductive".The *mouras encantadas* are shapeshifters and there are a number of legends, and versions of the same legend, as a result of centuries of oral tradition. They appear as guardians of the pathways into the earth and of the "limit" frontiers where it was believed that the supernatural could manifest itself. *Mouras encantadas* are magical maidens who guard castles, caves, bridges, wells, rivers, and treasures.

Having built our argument and hopefully de-constructed the illusion sufficiently at this point, the reader can take this one apart on their own. These stories are global. We often listen with slightly dreamy attention when a professor or intellectual points out that most of the global myths are the same myth. We nod along in agreement that it is quite the coincidence and perhaps there is something to it! We are never allowed to draw the logical conclusion that once, first, there was a global community which worked very well in concert with the earth and what is natural to her to create in ways we would now consider mystifying and magical or, even more likely, in ways that never really happened at all. Just our Imagination. Merely the archetypes and the collective unconscious representing non-incidents, mere metaphors. I will say again and again that understanding and acknowledging the Fae is fundamental to regaining our true sense of just who we are. When we clearly know who we are and what we can do we will know who or what is working against us. (Let's start with the obvious choice: any entity seeking to hide our true history from us and/or destroy any pertinent artifact).

In the 'newer' parts of our modern world, we find entities such as White Buffalo Woman among the Native American tribes. She will reappear at the time of the Cleansing of the Earth, it is said. There are many false paths in research when it comes to finding legends of women in white and ancient cultures. One must fight one's way past feminist studies and ghost stories, for example. It is that way now with all the distractions firmly in place. Try investigating the Fae using the word fairy!

Finally, we begin to see these appearances chalked up to visions of the Mother Mary after the Catholic Church co-opted all and sundry. These have been on the menu in this way for centuries. Even the infamous sighting of Our Lady at Fatima came complete with a dazzling display centring around the sun on the last visit. What better calling card for Brigid?

Our Lady appears ever covered by a mantle. "Also long known as The Mistress of the Mantle, She represents the sister or *virgin aspect* of the Great Goddess...She possesses an unusual status as a Sun Goddess Who hangs Her Cloak upon the rays of the Sun and whose dwelling-place radiates light as if on fire." Brigid's role as Mother

Goddess was never completely eradicated and reappears throughout Her entire career as a Catholic saint. As Saint Brigid, there are rays of sunlight coming from Her head, as portrayed as a Goddess. Themes of milk, fire, Sun and serpents followed Her on this path, adding to Her ever-growing popularity. Compassion, generosity, hospitality, spinning and weaving, smithwork, healing and agriculture ran throughout Her various lives and evolution. Her symbolism as a Sun Goddess remains, also, in the form of Brigid's crosses, a widdershins or counter-clockwise swastika, found world-wide as a profound symbol, The cult of Mry is well-acquainted with her protective mantle.

In fact, I am convinced that the oft-depicted Mary standing on a World barefoot with a snake beneath her feet and twelve stars around her head is nothing more than the Fae depicted as vanquishing the Draco. Alternatively, it could well be Fae representing communication between the stars and the planet, or travelling between the stars and the planet, with the snake representing the flow of the Dragon Lines. Either way, the Fae have been presented as who they really are in that image. We are simply not allowed to know that any longer...

Chapter 5 – Twilight Language

We have our Imagination as the translator between what is in the morphogenic field, which has been called pure potential, and the material plane in which we live. We are, in fact, magical creatures.

The myth that states that the God of the Sea rose and covered the Tuatha de Danaan in a mist and relegated them to the underworld. Translation: The Catholic Church, worshippers to this day of the Cult of Dagon (The Fish God), through a mist (of lies and prevarication) over the Tuatha de Danaan, and absconded with their most powerful incantation. The Faidh Fiadha which first word is pronounced *faith*, assigning it then to the Entity of Conquest, Patrick, and the Fae were beaten back into the Unremembered. This is a very good example of a message hidden within a myth. This is twilight language, indeed.

In fact, this story we hear across the ages in so many cultures. A god of some sort banishes the culture in place to the underworld never to be seen again. It is a good idea to dismantle this somewhat all the while trying to keep from sliding down a few slippery slopes so well prepared for us. It is important to understand that our so-called unconscious has been used as a tool against us very much the same way that the archetypes and myths have. Relegating an even or image or fact to any of these bins is an easy way to place something only in the realm of abstract and eliminate it from the real. One does not cancel the other out. However, there is some serious straightening out to do here.

Let us begin with symbols. Yes, it is true that symbols certainly represent a kind of twilight language. Our swastika is a good example of this. Meanings can be easily changed when the passage of time combines with the will to distort. Jung would say that symbols themselves carry the meaning within them. I agree. Distorted symbols do make us very uncomfortable, as if we feel the mangled aura emanating from them. The sort of twilight language we are greatly concerned with here though deals with the layers of meaning kin, for example, a sentence. There can be several. There is face value, which has largely to do with the time and culture in which one lives. One can only apply that, naturally, to any communication one comes across. However, a bit of knowledge about a subject under discussion and sometimes another layer is plumbed. With each layer a bit of magic is released. Complete shifts in perception come in those instants wherein an utterly new meaning presents itself.

Yes, it is true that Jung postulated that all meaning was held in the subconscious, however one wants to name that. However, I contend there is meaning, power and magic in the words themselves, in the actual construction of word. This is one reason etymology and all of its various components are so useful. That, however, comes across as crusty and dry, like a mummy waiting to be unearthed. In fact, words have life. The Logos. We enliven them, particularly if they are spoken. We nail them down, alas, when they are written. And it is in that life that there is meaning, layers of such because we are creatures of magic, just waiting to be set free.

There are some definitions of Twilight Language that I think are worth considering, even if none of them on their own is quite a complete rendering of the layering possible. "Officially, Twilight Language is a polysemic language and communication system dealing with visual, verbal, and non-verbal communications within tantric Buddhism and Hinduism. In other words, it was a secret symbolic language of which only the initiates of these faiths would be able to understand. In theory, this language would have predated Sanskrit and may not have been written down initially.

Buddhism's tantras are thousands of years old and yet never publicly revealed, never written down. Gradually it became necessary to write the secrets down so they would not be completely lost. But when they were written in a 'twilight language,' that is, in allegory, symbolism, code, so they could not be misinterpreted and misused by unworthy seekers." [25] Naturally, this sort of tool would be picked up by any who wanted to keep things secret for in knowledge and exclusivity, there is power. "In secret societies, 'twilight language' was advertised as Adamic language, the language Adam learned from God in Eden, 'the key to divine

---

[25] Coleman, L. *The Copycat Effect.*

knowledge." [26] The entire concept of Twilight Language is fascinating. Is this the original form of communication, brought by and used by the Fae? If we assume that the originals on this planet created by vocalizing at magnetic power centres then any form of potency within the vocal utterance is possible, indeed, even probable. Coleman finishes with, **"Twilight Language concerns, from psychology, the hidden significance of locations, dates, and other signs, from religious studies, the hidden symbolism that lies in the texture of the incidents; and, from criminology, the profiling insights that have revealed the ritualistic nature of certain crimes and incidents..."** Certainly, my interest for our purposes in this book is to point out how language has been used to both hide and allow us to find.

A truly excellent example of Twilight Language and the layers of a statement are the Buddhist koans. In fact, it was through impartial analysis of such that the idea of Twilight Language was voiced again. My sense is that there may be a simple plan, something one can know to unlock the secrets of a language. That seems completely probable. However, there is also that which lives inside the human being which has already the primer for information coming. When the time is ripe and the person is ready, the secrets unlock themselves. So is it also an agreement between what's out there and what's in there? I have written prior about the incalculable

[26] Hoffman, M. *Secret Societies and Psychological Warfare.*

number of treasures hidden beneath the Vatican. They are there so that we may not be allowed to resonate with them. This is my belief.

Of course, we are also aware that history itself is not all the church wanted to fracture and eliminate. There was as much a war waged against women and against any who practiced non-Catholic cosmologies. We have tried to allow the argument that the culture of the Fae found itself expressed in largely feminine energy and feminine modes. For me, the church's commitment to wiping out any woman who seemed to have her own power is a validation of this theory.

Fairy tales themselves are a form of Twilight Language. We say that, for example, Grimm's Fairy Tales contain archetypes that are important for children to receive and that children are able to encounter these archetypes and gain something from them that is closed off to most adults. We see the face value. Children hear the living layers singing to them. Some would even say that is why they exist.

Chapter 7 – Angels or Demons: A Pirate's War

We have our Imagination as the translator between what is in the morphogenic field, which has been called pure potential,

and the material plane in which we live. We are, in fact, magical
creatures.

I was simply tempted to ask the question to the universe, so I did: what's the difference between a fairy and an angel? Most telling response? An Angel is immortal. A fairy dies if a middle class child refuses to clap their hands during the play. (Peter Pan, of course). I'd forgotten that Peter Pan came before Walt Disney. Tinkerbell was simply an easy target, an even easier code name, for the media moguls who came shortly on the heels of John Barrie. The truth is neither of those statements is even Shadow Language in the way that I mean it. They are cages. Prisons. We have areas of language which have been captured and very effectively shut down. This idea of the fairy as a degenerated version of the Fae is one. A true organically layered shadow language statement is quite free to reveal itself, if the reader has eyes to see and ears to hear.

I've added this chapter, not because I have any interest in either demons, or djinn, or archons, or so-called elves and fairies. Nor have I ever been tempted to confuse any one of them with another. I added this chapter because as soon as I started to speak and write seriously about the Fae, the opposition made itself known by way of scoffing where scoffing was profoundly unexpected and inappropriate and by way of relegating the notion of the Fae to the popular culture rubbish heap. Done and dusted. No difference between any of the above and they are all negative. This reaction is either a sign of fear, a sign of the opposition, or a sign of some very, very lazy thinking. Maybe it's all three.

I also became aware fairly early on that there was or is an artist out there who is convinced he is drawing images of the Fae. He is also convinced they force him to build portals for them. The images are, almost surely, of Djinn. And Fae have no need for any kind of portal. So, it is my hope that this fellow can disconnect himself from these forces as they do appear to be parasiting on him and making him very unhappy. The Fae are amoral, remember? They are here to protect the Apple Tree and really have little concern for the apples themselves. If an entity is forcing you to do something for them, please, this is not the FAE. Seek assistance immediately!

The fallout has been unexpected and strange. Indeed, it became very obvious as well that this work must be protected closely until publication and presentation. I will say here and now that my computer was hacked while writing this book; Maria Wheatley's computer and her laptop were both hacked; and previously trusted members of the community were suddenly presenting research, Maria's research, as their own just ever so slightly ahead of the reveal dates for various projects. It became a pirate's war indeed. And so as we came closer and closer to publication, we resorted to post and courier for ferrying work back and forth. At one point, I was not sure I should publish unless it was just a few hours before Maria and I gave the inaugural lecture. However, getting into this space gave me real drive to write about the negative entities and energies that the Fae are not. They, not the Fae, are present and hijacking human bodies, minds, souls and thoughts. Desire, envy, a longing for acclaim, a longing for validation and, frankly, just the ability to squeak out a living as an activist…these are powerful motives indeed. These are often the foundations of piracy. In terms of the archons, as opposed to the other two negative entities, they just want to generate negative emotional energy in us and feed off it. This is no more cunning than a tapeworm.

Let us begin by revisiting the idea that archetypes (as in arch-angel?) have been seriously discussed as potential candidates for possession in some forms of mental illness. I really don't like using the phrase 'mental illness,' as it is the case that all humans have been very carefully and methodically fashioned to create hollow spaces within in which malicious forces can nestle, reside and from which they can do business. This, I believe, was a deep postulate from Carl Jung. Archetypes is a splendid candidate, in fact, for Twilight Language analysis. Arch-angel. Arch-enemy. Arch-type. Arch meaning portal? *Arc de Triomphe*. Noah's Arc. The Arc of the Covenant. The archetypes. We say that to ourselves all the time: well, these are the archetypes and we all know them and understand them on a subconscious level.

The chief danger is that of succumbing to the fascinating influence of the archetypes, and that is most likely to happen when the archetypal figures, which are endowed with a certain autonomy anyway on account of their natural numinosity, will escape from conscious control altogether and become completely independent, thus producing the phenomena of possession...[27]

Possession via the archetype is not merely a threat to the mentally unstable but to entire societies who can be induced to mass madness via archetype identification. Nazi Germany stands as a fine example of this in the modern era. But tyrants throughout history have used this technique. The Roman Catholic church does it today by superimposing the idea of the *Matre* in the form of the Virgin Mary where the Fae are/should be. Anthropologist Joseph Campbell writes:

The highest concern of all the mythologies, ceremonials, ethical systems, and social organization of the agriculturally-based societies has been that of suppressing the manifestation of individualism; and this has been generally achieved by compelling or persuading people to identify themselves not with their own interests, intuitions, or modes of experience, but with the archetypes of behaviour and systems of sentiment developed and maintained in the public domain.[28] The Fae were not an agriculturally based

---

[27] Jung, C. *The Archetype and the Collective Unconscious*
[28] Campbell, J. Masks of God, Primitive Mythology.

society, as was supposedly manifested subsequent to Cain and Abel (Bres and Lugh).

When one looks into the archetypes, whether angel or demon, one cannot find much that has not been stewed in a pot by the Roman Catholics and the Jesuits. We strive in this work to unearth evidence from prior to the changing of the timeline by Pope Gregory. It remains exceedingly difficult. There is much to be determined and understood simply by this re-evaluation of the term archetype itself. If we think about the discourse over time, though, do we ever hear of or read about someone who has been possessed by an angel or an archangel? Not to my knowledge. However, we do have a wealth of lore regarding possession by demons, their antiquity and their malicious intent. In fact, I find no literature that indicates that a so-called demon can act independently of a host. 'Angels' and 'archangels' act independently of a human being. Further to that, I find no literature of any kind that suggests a Fae or even the non-reality of the fairy inhabits a human being, takes them over, and commits any acts whatsoever while in that human body or mind or psyche.

We do find the same sort of stories in quantity regarding the Djinn. The Djinn I can say with certainty that I have seen myself in the state of consciousness that exists between waking and sleeping. That is a realm, indeed. The Djinn shapeshift. The Djinn are a type of demon, perhaps, from the ancient Middle East. In fact, it seems to be the will which is absconded with when we discuss all of these supposed entities. The Djinn, demons, the archons…while there are stories aplenty about unlucky human beings who got in the way of what seems to me to be a ritual of protection of the earth's magnetic energy, ie the fairy paths and the raths one cannot interfere with, there are no stories of which I am aware in which the Fae took possession of a human being and steered his or her actions. The will, which is the focused magic, must be left intact when encountering the Fae. It seems to me that the derailing of the human will has absolutely nothing to do with the takeover and use of the Imagination, either. It seems to have to do with seeking out and vicariously enjoying that which is astral: appetites and desires.

Yes, there is lore attached to the Fae that has to do with stealing babies and replacing them with changelings. However, shape-shifting is a function of the Djinn, of all of the entities we can talk about here that, for lack of intellectual rigour, get lumped together as one illogically solidified mass of negative qualities. Additionally, the High People had faded from the popular mindset long before, I think, the *fairies* began to be seen as a malevolent baby-stealing entity. We have also got to contend with the Dark Magic on our planet, the black forces working even today, and the targeting of children. It would be quite convenient to make that an historical act of the Fae. I do not believe it to be the case at this time nor do I believe that the actual Fae are responsible for so-called abductions. It seems quite clear to me that there is ample evidence that abductions are carried out mostly by the military and the practitioners of both black magic and the requisite blood sacrifices on this planet.

One definition of demon I recently heard is unresolved energetic force that has attained consciousness.[29] These could be entities brought into our dimension against their will but I wonder…and even if, as some would have us believe, anything other than the physical manifestation we see as life right now this very minute is simply 'energetic wildlife' outside our visual spectrum, what then does that mean? Does it mean these entities have nothing whatsoever to do with us and never did? There could be some sense to that in regards to the Catholic Church, which when one looks at the true history and purpose of that political organization, might well capture a rogue entity for its own purposes and leave it here in our dimension to roam and pillage. Indeed, archontic interference might also convince many a mind that materializing a demonic energy on this plane would only be good for raising the 'food' on which an archon feasts. It would, then, be worthwhile to consider this cult of Rome and archontic institution.

It is likely that their visual spectrum is broader than ours at this point as ours is being tampered with and they can likely see us even if we, for the most part, cannot see them. The postulate that we need an atmosphere in which to see anything came to notice as one

---

[29] Sheridan, T.

of Viktor Schauberger's. Our atmosphere has been so changed in the 20th century that it is probable that we can no longer see in any of the ways we have done before. What then of the Catholic Church and its demons, potentially wildlife let loose upon us indeed with what could be nothing more than a real racket of so-called exorcisms which in essence would just move the rabid, unhappy beast along?

What of the Middle East and its Djinn? What of the archons which apparently can be seen in the infrared? And what of the Fae, deeply wedded and basically caring only for this planet, who can be seen when they want to be seen, assuming we still have the ability to do so? That's collectively a whole lot of self-movement and will for energetic wildlife.

So let us reiterate:

Archons. A parasitical infection, come from off-world and likely seen in the Middle East during some of, if not all, of the Crusades which emanated from that region. Co-opting our very thoughts such that a high level of negative emotion can be generated on which they feed. Likely the movers and shakers behind the current Catholic Church. Still, a very simple organism and, in the end, easy to chase off with proper thought exercises. Can be seen and photographed in the infra-red spectrum.

Demons. According to some, these are 'energetic wildlife' living in a completely different dimension and brought here against their will, trapped. Probably collected and set loose by the archontically-controlled Catholic Church as a very effective generator of high negative emotion. Could be seen as the fertilizer on archontic crops and a symbol enabling real control over people by the church, as the church claims to be the sole authority able to dispel them. In fact, a dispelled demon is simply moving off to another space, if this theory holds water, unless returned to its proper dimension.

Djinn. **In the Koran and Muslim tradition, a spirit often capable of assuming human or animal form and exercising supernatural influence over people. Arabic jinnī,** *demonic,* *demon,* **from jinn,** *demons,* **from janna,** *to cover, conceal*

Usage Note: According to the Koran, humans share this world with another race of mortal beings, the jinn, that God created from pure, smokeless fire and endowed with supernatural powers. In Arabic, the noun *jinn* **designates these beings as a group.** [30]

Fae. (A definition, as parallel to the other definitions as possible, of fairy). **The word "fairy" derives from the Latin** *fata,*

---

[30] *American Heritage® Dictionary of the English Language, Fifth Edition.* S.v. "djinn."

and is from the Old French form *faerie*, describing "enchantment". Other forms are the Italian *fata*, and the Provençal "fada". In old French romance, "fee" was a woman skilled in magic, and who knew the power and virtue of words, of stones, and of herbs...According to King James in his dissertation Daemonologie, the term "faries" was used to describe illusory spirits (demonic entities) that prophesy, consort, and transport individuals they served.[31]

The Real Definition of the word Fae: a member of one of, if the not the primary, seed race which arrived on this planet potentially around 40,000 BC. Inhabited the area pof the world we now know as Ireland and its descendants spread across the planet creating cultures and civilizations of such a similar and lasting nature that each could only be considered as part of one people.

This is not demon. This is not Djinn. This is not Archon.

There are a class of negative entities we must consider, I think, before we leave this short chapter. We must consider them and wonder from whence they spring. One, the fear of the creative spirit; two, the fear of revelation; and three; lazy thinking. Collectively, these represent an entropy that will keep us from discovering who we truly are and every adversary

---

[31] https://en.wikipedia.org/wiki/Fairy

knows this. Therefore, it is anything we encounter which causes us to remain inside this 'cave' that we must really name demon.

#

Sacred Sites and the Sidhe

by Maria Wheatley

The Sidhe (shee) are considered to be a distinct race completely separate from human beings and numerous testimonies support this. Despite the dominant control of Christian power, belief in this race of beings that have supernatural powers far beyond those of mortal men and women has persisted across the centuries. The Fae have never gone away! Some say they move quickly through the air, can shape shift at will and are intimately associated with prehistoric sacred sites.

It is said that when the first Gaels, the sons of Mil, arrived in Ireland, they found that the Tuatha De Danaan, the people of the goddess Dana, controlled the land. The sons of Mil fought them in battle and defeated them, driving them 'underground' where it is said they remain to this day in the hollow hills or sidhe mounds. If I use this statement as a general fact *driving them underground into the sidhe or mounds,* which is mooted over and over again, we can time the event as most mounds are dated to either the Neolithic or the Bronze Age. Using the standard archaeological dating sequence, some mounds, like Newgrange, date to 3800-3400 BC., which allow us to pinpoint, and calculate, a time frame for the departure of the Tuatha De Danaan. Undoubtedly, if the latter mounds were the main focus, then 2500-2000 BC is the time phase.

Furthermore, held sacredly within the early Irish manuscripts are references to the Tuatha De Danaan. In *The Book of the Dun Cow* and *The Book of Leinster* this race of beings is described as *gods and not gods* pointing to the fact that they are something different, something supernatural. *The Book of the Dun Cow* informs us that the Tuatha De Danaan came from heaven, on account of their intelligence and excellence of their knowledge.

The Harrowing of the North

All things *Celtic* seem to focus on Ireland, Wales, Scotland and parts of Cornwall. The majority of counties in England escape Celtic Heritage or association. Apart from King Arthur, and a description of the great Kings of England by Geoffrey of Monmouth, there is a distinctive absence of 'English-Celtic' myths and legends. This was due to the *Harrowing of the North.*

The Harrowing of the North

The Harrying or Harrowing of the North was a series of campaigns waged by William the Conqueror in the winter of 1069–70 to subjugate northern England. Sacred texts and manuscripts that versed England's holy Celtic history were believed by some to be housed in the strongholds, cathedrals, and abbeys of the northern England. Wessex leader, Edgar Atheling, had encouraged Anglo-Danish rebellions that broke the Norman hold on the North. However, William paid the Danes to go home and the remaining rebels refused to meet him in battle. Instead, they decided to starve them out by laying waste to the northern shires, especially the city of York, before installing a Norman aristocracy throughout the region.

Medieval chronicles vividly record the savagery of the campaign, the huge scale of the destruction and the terrible widespread famine caused by looting, burning and slaughtering. Crops were burnt and men, women and children starved to death amid the wastelands of the north. Once thriving market towns became ghost towns as death replaced life and silence replaced the bustling noises of the towns and villages. Historical manuscripts, myths, legends and stories were said to be destroyed in the unforgiving and relentless slaughter. English Celtic scripts, probably containing the names, locations and meanings of their deities, gods and goddesses, had been destroyed forever. Due to the Harrowing, the English have no national Celtic identity; except in our Souls. The English are Celtic too, and the land testifies to this, as England has some of the largest Druidic Cors (colleges and universities) in the British Isles as well as numerous

Druidic ceremonial centres. Oxford University was sited above a Druidic Cor as it is said to be the esoteric centre of England and underneath the city, a red dragon and a white dragon were buried. Stories contain esoteric traditions and have a life of their own.

Ancient Sites

Stories open us to the magic of the Earth and they can reconnect us to it. A mound in Marlborough truly comes to life when we know its holy history and that this is where the Magician Merlin is said to be buried.

Ancient sites, such as the stone circles, mounds and the Celtic Fae forts are a physical link to our ancestral past. These sacred locations, especially the earthen mounds, were the chosen destination of the Tuatha De Danaan and they still remain power places. Interestingly, time-lapse experiences are intimately associated with the enigmatic mounds. It is said that sometimes humans were lured into their fairylands, there to be entertained for what seemed a short while, only to find on returning home that a hundred years of our time had passed.

Stories are common of youths that have entered the Fae realms have returned only to find their there beloved clean kept home ivy-clad and ruinous as decades had passed. Others have met their great grandchildren and then suddenly disintegrate into black ashes. Stories abound giving the earthen mounds and sacred sites a mystical power that transcends time and space.

At these timeless locations, we can reconnect to the Earth, to the Spirit of Place and to our ancestors. Deep below most sacred sites is pure water, often in the form of a lake and as water has memory, we can connect to the esoteric and actual history of the site. Deep waters emit electromagnetic energy and my research has shown that numerous ancient sites were purposefully sited above a particular type of water which I call *Yin* Water.

Sacred yin water

Nearly a century ago, it was noted that *blind springs* were found at the heart of an ancient site. A blind spring produces primary water. I was taught that primary water is alive, feminine, healing, and sacred. I call this water *yin water*, as it is produced chemically deep within Mother Earth and it is completely independent of rainfall (yang water). Internally, the Earth continually produces primary yin water and so a blind spring will never run dry. Pressure forces the yin water upwards through vertical fault lines and when it eventually reaches the surface, it is revered as a 'sacred spring' and often where it was bored defined a Holy Well.

Underground yin water produces an intense electromagnetic energy field and emits a spiral pattern. When dowsers such as myself locate this energy pattern, we know it is the location of deep underground yin water.

Ancient people used the geometric spiral energy as a design canon for the positioning of stone circles and often erected standing stones above it. The spiral pattern is called a 'geospiral' that consists of magnetic coils that can manifest in multiples of 7. According to the Master Dowser, Guy Underwood, whose unpublished manuscripts and earth energy surveys I inherited, the Earth energy geospiral motif inspired prehistoric artists to carve spiral patterns upon stones, ivory and other objects. To prehistoric people the spiral pattern has always been closely associated with water and the ceremonial way to approach a spiritual dimension. The geospiral pattern marks the esoteric centre of a site.

A 7-coiled geospiral pattern and a carved spiral motif

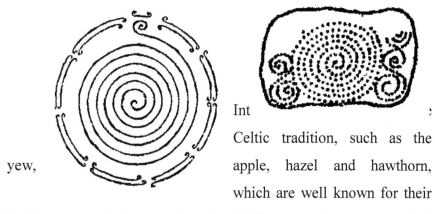

yew, Int Celtic tradition, such as the apple, hazel and hawthorn, which are well known for their healing or magical properties, invariably grow above a geospiral. The Druids were renowned for their in-depth understanding of Nature, and no doubt, these ancient masters fully understood the esoteric significance of the geospiral pattern and integrated it into their rituals and ceremonies. To the Aborigines of Australia a decorative spiral pattern, very similar to the geospiral motif, signifies a well or an underground water source and is deemed a sacred location.

> *When I was learning esoteric water divining I was taught that sacred healing springs and holy wells renowned for their medicinal properties are invariably sited above the geospiral pattern, indicating a prominent source of yin water. Yang water emits a distinctive pattern and an inharmonious energy field. Long-term exposure to this field is injurious to health, whereas, yin water emits a harmonic healing field. Both types of water are safe to drink.*

All water has memory; this is a fundamental principle of holistic practices such as homeopathy. Large volumes of pure yin water that are found deep beneath a sacred site contain the site's Holy History. Using mediation we can attune and tap into the Water's Akashic Records and explore time past. Just by sitting above the pattern and asking for permission to connect to the deep waters allows a relationship to be born. Go to the near centre of any ancient site and you will be in close proximity to a geospiral and its deep inner waters.

The ancient sites that I have compiled for this book are not the famous tourist attractions, such as Stonehenge or Avebury Henge in Wiltshire, England. They are quiet, divine and holy places with a True Spirit of Place touches and stirs the Soul into remembering that which was and what will be again. At these places, the unseen Earth energy naturally takes us from the ordinary into the extraordinary.

When we gently and lovingly ask for permission to interact with the energies of the site, all kinds of wonders can happen.

Stoney Littleton long barrow – land of the Fae

Going back twenty-five years or so ago, when I was a young geomancer dowser, my late father, a family friend and I visited Stoney Littleton long barrow. According to the prolific authors, Janet and Colin Bord, this long barrow was said to be home to the fairy folk.

We arrived at the long barrow in an autumnal mist adding a natural magic to the day. However, due to unstable masonry the entrance to the barrow was barred with an iron gate denying us access. Today, the barrow is fully restored and always open to the wandering spiritual pilgrim. We dowsed the barrow for healing areas, which were surveyed by the Master Dowser Guy Underwood over 60 years ago, which are marked as small spiral areas in the following illustration. Years later, I would discover that these small spirals are often associated with the outpourings of negative ions which are beneficial to our health. We also located leys, and Earth energies and then made our way back down the hill to return to the car. Half way down the hill I realised I had left my dowsing rod near the barrow's entrance and ascended the hill once more to retrieve it.

I picked up the rod and felt saddened that I could not enter the barrow. Several stones required resetting making the inner chambers unstable and dangerous. I was just turning to leave when a creaking sound caught my attention. I looked towards the entrance and the iron gate was now open!

I had no hesitation; I was going in. Even today when you enter Stoney Littleton you usually take a torch. This is because you have crawl on your hands and knees along a long gallery that is 16 meters long and only 1 meter high. The crawl is worth it as three pairs of energy-filled chambers and a far chamber are waiting to greet you. It was pitch black, I crawled along this seemingly never-ending gallery, and it was musky and damp. Reaching the far chamber, I turned around to face the light and the entrance. I saw tiny sparks of dancing white light, swirling and hypnotic. I was transfixed. After a short while the small lights faded and were gone, I crawled back and rushed down the hill. I spoke of my little adventure and dad said: 'But Maria, it was pad-locked!' Puzzled I tried to make sense of my experience. Our family friend jokingly said, 'Perhaps the fairies wanted to show you something!' I think they did.

Stoney Littleton long barrow, Wellow, Somerset. A Neolithic horned long barrow dated to c3800 BC. Aligned to face the Winter Solstice sunrise this barrow is the finest in Somerset. A ley courses down the axis line and healing energy spots are marked as small spirals in the following survey. This is where Earth energy rises to the surface and generates a gentle healing vortex effect.

STONEY LITTLETON SURVEY BY UNDERWOOD.

Negative ions rise from the small spirals

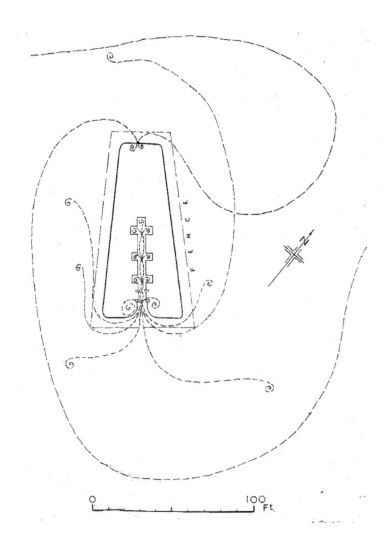

Stanton Drew stone circles, Stanton Drew, Somerset.

In the 1940s, a strange Otherworldly event was recorded for

prosperity and the setting was the Great Stone Circle of Stanton Drew. Whatever actually happened on this day is hard to say but something mysterious did occur and the witness was of impeccable character.

It was just another dull and cloudy day when Major F.A. Menzies, a distinguished WWI engineer and surveyor, saw an event that was about to change his life. He kept it a secret, probably in fear of ridicule, until one year before his death.

'Although the weather was dull and there was no sign of a storm, just at a moment when I was re-checking a [compass] bearing in that group, it was as if a powerful flash of lightning hit the stone, so the whole group was flood-lit, making them glow like molten gold in a furnace. Rooted to the spot – unable to move – I became profoundly awestruck, as dazzling radiations from above caused the whole group of stones to pulsate with energy in a way that was terrifying. Before my eyes, it seemed the stones were enveloped in a moving pillar of fire – radiating light without heat –writhing upwards towards the   heavens; on the other hand it was descending in a vivid spiral effect of various shades of colour – Earthward. In fact the moving, flaring lights gyrating around the stones had joined the heavens with the Earth.'

Stanton Drew is a magical place which has three individual and inviting stone circles. The Great Circle has 36 stones and is 368 feet in diameter making it the second largest stone circle in the world; second only to Avebury Henge's outer circle. The northeast circle is 97 feet in diameter close to Stonehenge's sarsen circle diameter. Eight massive pink coloured stones up to 9 feet high stand elegantly and draw your attention. The eight stones mark the eight years and the 99 full moons of the Venus pentagram cycle making this circle feminine.

The Northeast circle of eight stones and the Venus pentagram.

The SSW ring is 147 feet across and once contained 12 standing stones and is said to be the *Temple of the Moon*. This ring  of stone is sited upon a hill, overlooks the other two circles, and seems to guard the landscape below. Nearby, in is a Cove feature in the Druid's Inn beer garden!

 The Cove may have been a long barrow and it marks a source of earth energy called a Crown chakra geospiral. A church dedicated to St Mary can be seen aligned to the Cove Stones.

The Cove Stones

Remnants of the stone avenues.
Rich in iron, which is a great conductor, the stones have immense energy.

 Once two avenues joined the circles, which you can see in the illustration. Im the summer of 2016, I took two American authors to Stanton

Drew called Pia and Cullen Orlean. We were interacting with the avenue stones – feeling and touching them – when suddenly I felt heat radiating from a stone and yet it was a windy and damp summer's day. The heat was astonishing and unmistakable and another avenue stone also emitted a heat force that could clearly be felt. Pia and Cullen also felt that some of the avenue stones were hot whilst some were emitting a cool energy. Stanton Drew is extraordinary.

Merry Maidens, Cornwall

Standing neatly like a Fairy Ring this granite stone circle was fully restored in the 1860s. Nineteen stones form a perfect circle 78 feet (23.8 metres) in diameter. Each stone is around 4 feet high and rectangular in shape. Close by, a second circle may have once existed but sadly nothing remains of it today. A quarter of a mile away from this feminine womb like circle is a pair of stones called the Pipers. The north east pillar is 15 feet tall and its partner is 13 feet high. A cup marked chambered tomb called Tregiffian is located by the road downhill to the west of the circle.

Dowsing as accurate as carbon dating

The late, and the greatest pendulum dowser in the world, Tom Lethbridge, dowsed the Merry Maidens with his long-cord pendulum method. Long cord pendulum dowsing uses a set 'rate' – length of cord – for dowsing a particular object. According to Tom *Age* was set at the rate of 30 inches. Using this length, he got the date of 2540 BC. Stranger still, he noted the pendulum swung so strongly it was horizontal. More than that, his hand resting on the stone received an intense electric shock. The stone which weighted around a ton felt to Tom as if it were rocking, moving and dancing.

The male stones close to the Merry Maidens

Druid Initiation chambers

Cornwall contains

several Druidic sites. The Druids were the priestly caste of the Iron Age (c700 BC – AD 43) and they thrived throughout the Celtic British Isles until the Roman legions committed an act of genocide and wiped them out. One of their constructs was a deep underground chamber called a fogou.

One of the finest examples of a Druid Fogou is **Halliggye Fogou** on the Lizard Peninsula in Cornwall. Situated on the Trelowarren Estate, this ancient site is now a little visited tourist attraction, which is open between April to September. 'Fogou' derives from the Cornish for cave (fogo).

Some archaeologists classify these structures as:

'Iron Age defensive structures found within fortified structures throughout Cornwall, northern Scotland and the Orkney Islands. Their function is unknown, though possibilities include refuge and food storage'.

Most of these structures are non-defensive and nor were they used for food storage as no evidence can verify this. These mysterious fogou constructs that descend deep into the Earth are ceremonial temple spaces or initiation chambers.

Inside A Fogou

Step inside a fogou and look around. The care that has been taken to create this construct is everywhere. Look at the walls and you will see perfect stonework, touch them to reconnect to the past and feel their smoothness. Now look to the zenith of the construct and you will notice that the walls taper towards the top and are capped by stone slabs. The workmanship of the corbelled roof creates a symmetry that is breathtaking. After you have looked around; still your mind and body by taking a couple of deep, slow breathes and you will sense an energy that is truly amazing.

Calling the Awen, calling for creativity.

To the Druids, the Holy Spirit is everywhere. This spiritual force was, and still, is called Awen. Throughout modern Western culture, inspiration is often viewed as an elusive, fleeting moment of awareness, accessible only to certain people such as artists, poets or inventors. To Druids, awen is the divine flowing spirit of inspiration and creativity; it is everywhere, within and around us. Awen is sacred.

Like water, the essential quality of awen is that it flows as it is *fluidic*. So, when it is accessed it is not to be hoarded in secret, or it will stagnate. To connect with it, and draw from it the energy we need for our own creative activities, all that is required is intent.

Awen is like the breathe of the universe and we can breathe it in, drawing upon the positive creative energy and then we can breathe it out again giving it to the world as a poem, or however you wish to express it. The flowing, creative spirit of awen can be accessed through chanting the word itself within a sacred space such as a fogou. We can call upon awen as it is a living and energetic spiritual force.

Druids cast a circle of power, often with their minds, by sensing a circle of beautiful white or golden light and within this protective space intent is set. To call the inspirational force of the universe, just sit comfortably and focus on your breathing. Take a deep breath and chant Aaaaaaa-ooooooo-eeeeee-nnnnnn, extending each sound, using the air in your lungs, chant with love and a sense of sacredness. Take a second breath and repeat the chant, then a third.

In Druid group rites, the word 'awen' is often chanted three times. However, in your own space, you may chant it as many times as you need to or what simply feels right. According to the British Druid Order, experiment with pitch and vibration. Lower pitch will affect the lower body, and a higher pitch will resonate in your chest or head. Experience the various pitches and discover which resonates with you.

As you chant, open your mind to whatever impressions come to you. Druids have experienced the presence of awen in many guises, as colours, lights, animal or plant forms, music, or as a sense of time and space beyond the 'normal three-dimesional world'.

Halliggye Fogou is an excellent place to call in the awen as it is a Druidic site It is one of 12 known surviving fogous in Cornwall. Originally, it was associated with the Earthworks of an Iron Age agricultural community. In 1982, after routine ploughing breached the roof of the main chamber it was excavated. The breach has now been converted into an entrance for visitors with new steps leading down.

Within the fogou there is a straight chamber set upon a 20 metres north-south axis line that terminates in a filled-in exit that used to come out in a ditch. Close to the far end a 28 metres long, gracefully curving side passage runs westwards ending with a short south facing *creep.*

All the descriptive writing in the world cannot replace the heighten feeling that a fogou gives. So the next time you are in Cornwall, I suggest that you visit one of the many underground chambers that descend deep into the Earth. Undoubtedly, they were dedicated to

Mother Earth, and they are a sacred place to experience the powerful Earth energies that imbue the site.

Carn Euny near Sancreed, Cornwall

Carn Euny lies on the Penwith peninsula in Cornwall. It is a well-preserved fogou with an underground passageway, which is approximately 65 feet (20 metres) long. The inner passageway runs just below the surface of the ground and is roofed with massive stone slabs.

Fogou energy can help you to make transformative changes in your life. You can enter a fogou as *yourself*, but you will leave feeling 'differently', If I feel that I need to make a change in my life and for whatever reason I am resisting that change– be that a state of mind, emotion or health, job etc – fogou energy will always assist with its natural strong alchemic force. I always bow to the fogou entrance before I enter to honour it, as fogous take us into the womb of the Earth, to the Otherworld and upon leaving offer us rebirth, such is its innate phoenix like power.

Mine Howe, Tankerness, Orkney.

One of the most powerful underground Druid chambers that I have visited is Mine Howe on the spectacular Isle of Orkney. Early in

1946, an excavation was carried out at an earthen mound in Tankerness known as Mine Howe. Hidden for thousands of years was a deep rock-built chamber which was wrongly interpreted as the remains of an Iron Age broch and the excavation was then filled in again.

Half a century passed, until one day the underground chamber called for our attention once more. 1999 was the year of the total solar eclipse, which could be seen from Cornwall and it reactivated some of Cornwall's fogous.

In  that year, the site of Mine Howe reacted to the solar eclipse force and its energies began to stir. Douglas Paterson, a local farmer, must have sensed Mine Howe 'calling' as he cleared out the chamber once more and to his atonishment rediscovered an entrance and found a passage that sank nearly vertically into the ground. It was accessed by 29 steep stone steps, which is a lunar number. Half way down, the air changes, it becomes more electric and heightens your sensitivity to the Spirit of Place. Interestingly, at this midpoint, the steps double back on themselves at a *landing*, and at the bottom there is a very deep step into the bottom of the chamber. Two long low galleries extended outwards from the half way *landing*.

The side galleries from the landing are easy to miss as you descend so remember to stop and look around. Once in the cistern, or foot of the structure, the energy changes dramatically as you find that natural light and sound from the entrance can no longer be seen or heard. You are now in the silent Otherworld, with the seen and the unseen spirits and your experience will be unforgettable.

Entrance to Mine Howe

Mine Howe was originally surrounded by a massive causewayed ditch that separated the sacred from the profane outer regions.

Sunkenkirk or Swinside Circle, Cumbria.

Swinside Circle was constructed about c3200 BC making it potentially one of the earliest in the country.

In total there are more than 300 stone circles in Britain, the great majority of them are Bronze Age which tend to be smaller than their earlier Neolithic cousins. The Neolithic megalithic culture constructed large stone circles such as Avebury Henge, Stanton Drew, Castlerigg, Long Meg and her Daughters in the Eden Valley, and the Ring of Brodgar in Orkeny as well as the breathtaking Celtic Cross stone circle called Callanish.

Out of the 60 stones believed to have made up this stone circle 55 remain with 30 still standing making this one of the most complete and unspoilt stone circles in the world. Standing facing the north, the pagan quadrant of power, is the tallest stone being about 2.3 metres in height. Retaining its circular shape and with no stones set in

concrete, like the restored stone circles of Avebury, Stonehenge, and the Merry Maidens, a natural energy fills the circle that makes you sense its omnipresent circular power.

The reason why Swinside is such an intact stone circle is that it stands nearly a mile from a small back road. The site itself consists of 93.8 feet (28.6 metres) in diameter of porphyritic slates. The entrance in the southeast is marked by two large outer portal stones and with an azimuth of 134°5 and a declination of -24°6 it is very close to the Winter Solstice sunrise.

At the turn of the 20th century, a small excavation revealed that the area had

been levelled prior to the erection of the stones. The name Sunkenkirk comes from a legend that the Devil pulled down the stones each night as the circle was being built.

I climbed the 'Mother Mound' close to the stones and felt that this was a ceremonial hill born of nature which was used by our ancestors. This landscape has a quite beauty that takes you back to former times and soothes the urban mind by reawakening ancient collective memories.

Castlerigg, near Keswick, Cumbria.

Set against a backdrop of beautiful mountains this stone circle is wondrous. Enter the stone circle like our ancestors did by walking around to the north side and you will see that it was flanked by two massive upright stones. The outlier is presently to the west-south-west of the stone circle, on the west side of the field adjacent to a stile, as it has been moved from its original position.

The diameter is close the Merry Maidens and the Venus stone circle of Stanton Drew, as it measures close to 97.5 feet (30 metres). Originally, it consisted of around forty-two stones but there are now only thirty-eight stones, which vary in height from 3 1/4 ft (1 m) to 7 1/2 ft (2.3 m).

Within the circle there is a rectangle containing a further 10 stones, which is an unusual feature as there is only one other comparable example, at the Cockpit, an open stone circle at Askham Fell, near Ullswater.

An Unusual Alignment

If you want to see a long lost design feature incorporated into Castlerigg, go there for the midsummer sunset and you will not be disappointed. Researcher John Glover discovered that the tallest stone in the ring casts an incredible shadow-line. He surveyed the line and found that it extended for approximately 3 km (2 miles) and that ancient sites were set along the axis. A fundamental aspect of the Old Religion was to encode their stone temples with a solar alignment that produced a dramatic shadow effect, which infused the land with solar power. This ancient rite gave a visual awareness of the intimate relationship between man, the heavenly sun and the ebb and flow of the ceremonial year.

Long Meg and her Daughters, close to Eden Valley, Cumbria

Long Meg and Her Daughters is the third largest stone circle in England. It consists of 70 remaining stones which were set in a large flattened oval. Two large stones mark the cardinal points of East and West and align to the Equinoxes.

Mother Nature saved this stone circle. In the eighteenth century, an attempt was made to destroy it by blasting, but thunderstorms and superstitions caused the work to stop.

The ancestral way of walking into this stone circle is through the entrance in the southwest, which is flanked by a pair of stones just outside the circle. When you walk into a sacred site in the way it was designed, you are flowing with the energetic foundation – the Earth energies that set the stone features and the feeling can be uplifting.

At Long Meg, an underground flowing female yin stream courses along the avenue. It was mentioned earlier that the deep inner waters born of Gaia are pure and they can store the memories of the site – all that was. Set the right intent and you can tap into the Water's memory field and sense time past or the timeless wisdom or the healing energy field that water emits.

Long Meg is pictured in the photograph. She is tall red sandstone that stands 3.8 metre tall and 82 feet 25 metres from the entrance. If you stand in the centre of the circle and look towards Long Meg, you will notice that she aligns to the midwinter sunset. The red hues of the setting sun enhance her colour as the waning light touches the megalithic. Old folklore says that she will bleed if you break a piece is off, so leave her alone, as she is not to be possessed. I love standing against her with my spine touching her - an exchange of energies which instantly balances your chakra system.

Look carefully at Long Meg as she holds yet another beauty. On the edge that faces the circle there are a series of rock carvings consisting of cups, rings, grooves, spirals and concentric circles. Although it is uncertain when these marks were made - after the stone had been erected - or whether Long Meg was cut out of an existing decorated rock outcrop, only Meg knows. But does it really matter? Because when you touch these sacred symbols, you are transcending time and reconnecting to your spiritual Celtic heritage, which is far more important than academic numbers that are proved by carbon dating in some sterile university lab. Sometimes to touch is to feel and to know. Long Megs calls us to touch.

According to John Aubrey writing in the mid 17th century, there were two large cairns inside the ring covering a 'Giants bone and Body'. But by the 18th century, they had been removed. Meg was probably a witch that is to say a wise woman and a Seer.

Although long gone, to the west of the circle aerial photography revealed the former existence of a Cursus monument which is earlier than the circle.

Callanish stone circle

Callanish stone circle stands tall in the Outer Hebrides on the Isle of Lewis,

Scotland. With a lay out similar to a Celtic cross, Callanish has a unique design. Callanish has many celestial alignments, but one stands out as a visual wonder and it is a sight to behold. Nowhere else on Earth will you see such a truly mesmerising lunar alignment. An event so rare that it must have been high on the Neolithic bucket list. The stones were saved from destruction as they were partly buried in peat until 1875 when they were dug out.

Margaret Curtis is a must have guide for Callanish as her knowledge of the site is incredible and her love for the stones even greater. Margaret rediscovered a long lost celestial alignment and I went there in 2006 to see it.

Margaret discovered that stone circle is connected to a feminine hill range which forms the body of a woman lying on her back. Local people call her 'Sleeping Beauty' or in Gaelic 'Cailleach na Mointeach' which translates as 'The Old Woman of the Moors.' Multiple prehistoric stone circles in the area were positioned to face Sleeping Beauty. But the visual wonder is the divine relationship between the Callanish stones, Sleeping Beauty and the Moon.

Every 18.61 years when the Full Moon is at its most southerly extreme position a breathtaking event begins. Visualise this, a bright honey coloured full moon is very low on the horizon, as if touching the Earth, as it rises over the breast of the

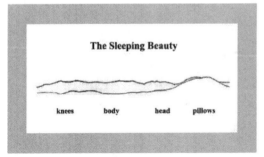

The Sleeping Beauty

knees   body   head   pillows

'Sleeping Beauty'. Slowly the Moon glides along her body and the contours of the hill make the bright full Moon disappear and reappear maximising the forthcoming drama.

Approximately 2-5 hours later, the Moon will pass through the Callanish stone circle in a way that will astound you. I suggest you stand along the avenue for the best view. At moonset when the bright orb passes through the central Callanish stones, if a person stands on the rocky hillock at the higher southern end, the moon dramatically reappears. Let us imagine a Neolithic priestess standing in this exact position 5000 years ago, waiting for this one moment in time as she knew something magical was about to happen.

Margaret calculated that when a priestess (or priest) stood in this position, she would appear silhouetted *within* the Moon. Perhaps she would sit inside of the moon, or a male and female would embrace one another. The beauty of this lunar event is endless. After a short time, the moon vanishes and leaves the person/s alone inside the silent and now darkened circle but forever remembered as being

within the Moon. Contact Margaret Curtis: on her web site:

http://www.geo.org/callan.htm.

In 2006, I never got to see the grand finale. But I did witness the Moonrise and the bright low amber orb glide across the body of the Sleeping Beauty, as if touching the hills to reawaken 'The Old Woman of the Moors'. That event kindled a deep love within me for the lost civilisation of Callanish and I thanked the ancestors, as well as the Moon, for a night that I would never forget...

Ireland. The Home of the Fae

Carrowkeel cairns and Cassiopeia

> *E.A. James Swagger is a leading authority on Ireland's ancient sites and he is at the forefront of megalithic*

research. The following celestial alignments and astronomical calculations, regarding the Carrowkeel Cairns and Newgrange, are extracted with kind permission, from his book 'The Newgrange Sirius Mystery. Linking Passage Grave Cosmology with Dogon Symbology'. His outstanding work gives us immeasurable insight into Ireland's Neolithic and Bronze Age heritage. www.megalihtcodyssey.com www.megalihitctv.com

Carrowkeel Cairns

The Carrowkeel Cairns are one of my favourite sacred sites. Dramatically placed on the side of a mountain, the cairns are positioned with solar, lunar and stellar accuracy. The elevated views give you a sense of wonderment, instantly transporting you from your daily life to a forgotten time. The sunlight upon the water, captured in this photograph, sparkles like diamonds giving the landscape a richness that money cannot buy.

There

are

three

main

cairns

that beckon the spiritual pilgrim to enter and you won't be disappointed. Created out of fine white quartz, these high resonance chambers are alive and full of crystal energy. E.A. James Swagger discovered that the cairns were purposefully aligned to a distinctive constellation. More than that, he uncovered proof that the ancient megalithic builders of Carrowkeel had an advanced knowledge of precession, which he calls *monitoring of precession*. Monitoring of precession is literally tracking an entire constellation across the sky.

Carrowkeel and Cassiopeia

Long before the cairns were raised, the prehistoric astronomers were monitoring the constellation of Cassiopeia in the night sky. The Romans saw Cassiopeia as being chained to a throne for her boastfulness and in Greek mythology she is the Queen of Ethiopia, the wife of Cepheus and the mother of Andromeda. To the Arabian

astronomers she was pictured as a kneeling camel.

Interestingly, some of the Irish deities reappear in Welsh literature. Parallel to the Tuatha De Dannan, although by no means identical, are the Children of Don. Some of the Welsh deities give their names to the constellations, such as Cassiopeia – Llys Don – meaning the Court of Don. Research author, Michael Bayley, suggests that to the Celts, Cassiopeia may have been seen as Don, the Mother of the Gods, or as Cerridwen who is still worshipped by modern day Druids and pagans. Certainly, Cassiopeia is visible all year round and as such may have been seen as immortal. Claudius Ptolemy, who studied at the Egyptian Library of Alexandra, informs us the rays of Cassiopeia command respect and gives boastfulness.

Cairns B,C,E,F and K are aligned to the stars of Cassiopeia when they set at the Winter Solstice. Photo shows Cairn G.

If we assume that Don is the Mother of the Gods, the cairns could represent the womb of the Goddess which may have been used as oracle chambers to contact the Great Goddess of the Sky. In myth,

Cerridwen was an adept shape shifter representing a three-fold system of Druidic initiation. Carrowkeel's inner chambers encourage our consciousness to 'shift' so like the great Celtic Goddess Cerridwen we can move through time and space.

On a more mathematical level, E.A. James Swagger notes that each star sets at a different time, so the ancients were 'obsessively tracking Cassiopeia'. Yet, there is symbolic beauty in Neolithic mathematics. The astronomers were watching for their setting location at the Winter Solstice, a time of the Solar year which symbolically represents the height of Goddess power. The Carrowkeel cairns were aligned to the eternal stars of Cassiopeia at a time when her celestial power and timeless wisdom was greatest.

The cairn chambers are incredible. When you are inside remember that you are looking at a design canon which is over five thousand years old. Touch the cool, pure white quartz walls and feel its splendour. Words cannot express the energy of this sacred space. The quartz gives sound energy work extra potency and even quite contemplation brings blissful contentment, as few people venture here, so the choice of what you do here will be yours.

On the outside, the cairns are equally stunning and were likewise finished off with white quartz, perhaps representing the white bright stars of Cassiopeia. Blending astronomical precision with captivating beauty, the stars last light aligned perfectly with the cairns just before their setting. Exactitude of this alignment to within 1 degree of accuracy is proof that the megalithic builders were Master mathematicians, engineers, and astronomers. Looking out of the cairn and seeing the setting star must have had a deep and profound meaning.

Cairn G is unique as it has a light box like Newgrange which captures the sun in one recess and also the moonset every 19 years. The slit in the stone diffuses the light entering the chamber creating an extraordinary Spirit of Place

There is also a spectacular Summer Solstice sunset alignment at Cairn G.

As late as the mediaeval period, Cassiopeia's influence had not totally ceased. In English churches, there is a dominance of M's and W's carved on walls, pillars and some seats. If we rule out initial name graffiti, we can ponder on a celestial meaning for its common occurrence. Most business transactions were made in churches, not just marriage contracts, but buying and selling, renting and payment of rents. It has been suggested by Michael Bayley that the Ms and Ws could represent the Quarter Days when rents were due which were timed by the presence of Cassiopeia in the night sky. At midsummer, Cassiopeia is in the W position, in the autumn it is in the position of a fallen W leaning to the left. In winter it is in the M position and by Spring it is the M fallen to the left. Payments and financial transactions were govern by this constellation and the season it governed.

Creevykeel Court Tomb

Creevykeel is amongst the finest examples of a full-court tomb in Ireland. The silver coloured stones sparkle in the sunlight and even under a damp or grey sky the stones seem to shine.

Dated to c3500 BC, this Neolithic tomb was excavated in 1935 and then it was restored. Four cremation burials, decorated and undecorated Neolithic pottery, flint arrowheads, polished stone axes and other artefacts, including a chalk ball were found. Trapezoidal in shape this temple space is about 50 metres in length.

Before you enter, take the time look and marvel at the front of the cairn which is about twenty metres across. Stepping inside you will notice that there is a narrow passage lined with orthostats, which calls you to step into a large oval court which is also lined with orthostats. Walk towards the north west of the monument and you will find a two chambered gallery. At the rear of the cairn there are three subsidiary chambers and each one feels feminine, healing or uplifting.

Court Tombs had a unique design. The roof did not fully cover the monument; a long narrow slit like line was left open. Usually the Court Tombs are orientated north-south as if pointing to the North Star. The forecourt area creates an astronomical observatory section at the entrance end. From here, with a clear horizon view you would be able to see the zenith and the stars passing overhead. In esoteric astrology, the star or planet that is located at the zenith of the birth chart activates the crown chakra. Perhaps, the forecourts were designed for crown chakra activation, at the very least the passing planet or star would be visible.

Newgrange – A Precessional Calculator?
By E.A. JAMES SWAGGER.
The Newgrange Precessional Calculator

Newgrange Passage grave is situated in the Boyne Valley complex of passage graves alongside its other two sister mounds of Knowth and Dowth. The Newgrange Passage tomb is the second closest to the Boyne River which one crosses over by foot from the visitor centre. Newgrange is a rather modern name, its Gaelic counterpart 'Brugh na Boinne' simply meaning a place name at the 'bend in the Boyne'. The Passage grave stands on a low-lying ridge over-looking the River Boyne and Red Mountain and the complex itself lies 8 km east of the town of Drogheda, County Louth.

The passage grave at Newgrange is estimated to be constructed about 3200 BC. This is often referred to as a kidney shaped mound or 'womb' shaped mound as some reference due to the sunbeam penetrating the passageway. The mound covers an area of over one acre and is surrounded by 97 kerbstones, most of which are richly decorated with megalithic art. Its size is approximately 95m by 85m in diameter giving it this 'heart' or 'kidney' shape. It is estimated that the construction of the Passage Tomb at Newgrange would have taken a work force of 300 at least 20 years though estimates widely vary and are highly speculative.

Historically, the Newgrange Passage grave first appears in 1699, where it was rediscovered during the removal of material to build a nearby road. It was Charles Campbell the local landlord who set his workers to remove stones which were conveniently at this mound that lay on his land. By chance they started their excavations on the south west side of the mound and uncovered the engraved lintel of the roof box. Soon after they had uncovered the entrance stone and for the first time since construction of the monument people re-entered the internal passageway and chamber of Newgrange. It wasn't until 1962 that a major excavation of Newgrange took place. This is when the sparkling white quartz façade was rebuilt using stone found at the site. Some believe it was actually not a façade and was in fact slippage as the mound was only topped in quartz, a style seen elsewhere throughout Ireland. It was most likely originally built in the shape of a truncated cone - like that of Dowth nearby, and like the unexcavated Maeve's Cairn and Heapstown Cairn of Sligo, Ireland. Nonetheless, it now sits pristinely on the landscape for all to awe and wonder of its function. Newgrange has now become a World Heritage Site which has been designated by UNESCO, attracting some 200,000 plus people a year.

Another unusual feature is the twelve standing stones that make an arc at the front of the mound; there may have been a complete circle of 35 or 36 stones, though not all the sockets have been found. Newgrange sits with four satellite mounds beside it, two to the east and two to the west. Two of these are buried today, the chamber of

one can be seen in the western adjacent field, and Cairn Z lies within the Newgrange enclosure to the east. Concrete pillars now replace the missing kerbstones of Site Z. The National Museum in Dublin displays some of the decorated stones from Cairn Z in the Passage Grave exhibit. The O'Kelly excavation revealed what appeared to have been a hut site outside the entrance. Encircling Site Z in the same compound as Newgrange sits the remains of a huge timber henge at about 90 meters, the same diameter of the Newgrange mound. Concrete stumps now mark some of these postholes.

The Newgrange Passage

Throughout the world, Newgrange is well known for its alignment to the Winter Solstice sunrise. Over the entrance, a shaft of sunlight is able to penetrate the passageway and thus the chamber. Cleverly, the passageway meanders so as to block the light from the entrance. The roof box has an undeterred path to the chamber. The entrance is also just the right height so that you slightly ascend as you meander through the very slightly inclined passageway. This way the passage and the beam of sunlight both meet in the awaiting chamber. The dramatic event lasts for 17 minutes on the morning of Winter Solstice and for a few days either side it. The 19-metre long inner passage leads to a cruciform chamber with a corbelled roof which still remains watertight today. On the shortest day of the year the Winter Solstice sunrise event at Newgrange is the most illustrious event in the Irish Cultural Calendar. There is a lot of media attention surrounding it nowadays and is usually filmed every year weather permitting.

Newgrange Passage Grave Plan and Internal Layout

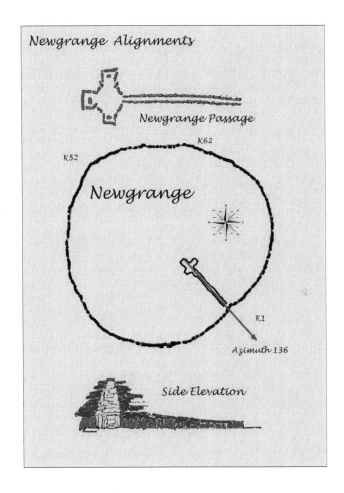

There is limited space inside but many gather outside to marvel at our ancient observational astronomers. The solar drama begins at dawn just after 9 am. Majestically, the sun begins to rise over Red Mountain and across the Boyne Valley where Newgrange is situated with its other sister sites of Knowth and Dowth. Just after four minutes past nine the front of the Newgrange monument is illuminated and the light enters the passage via the specially designed roof box. The beam of bright sunlight stretches into the passage of Newgrange and on into the central chamber for the next fourteen minutes. In Neolithic times, the rear stone was illuminated, but the light beam is now slightly off. It is remarkable that the ancients had such accuracy and planning for this spectacular event to survive the ages.

There are in fact two light beams as it is split from the doorway and light box. The doorway light beam is eventually drowned out by the meandering passage. The roof box light beam enters at about 34cm and narrows as it protrudes the long chamber. It is Orthostat (Upright Slab of Stone) C8 that captures the beam of light and it most likely reflected onto Orthostat C10 which contains the famous triple spiral motif.

Newgrange Internal Tri-Spiral

Passed from stone to stone, the light beam reaches its final destination and lights up the internal tri-spiral, Ireland's most icon symbol. Imagine seeing this event for the first time when Newgrange was pristine and fully functioning.

This is the same motif that lies on the entrance stone and is probably the most famous Irish Megalithic symbol. The internal tri-spiral design is about twelve inches and is about one third the size of the tri-spiral on the entrance stone. There are a plethora of theories on the entrance stone carvings but few if any link up the internal triple spiral with the outside one. The Newgrange Precessional Calculator Theory that I put forward here seems to not only link these triple spirals but shall explain the overall function of the monument as an intentional Precessional calculator albeit crude. Unfortunately, admission to the Newgrange chamber for the Winter Solstice sunrise is by lottery, as only a limited number of people can fit inside; some 20,000 people apply every year for 50 places.

The Alignments

Newgrange has other equally spectacular alignments. Created as an astronomical device, we have seen that Newgrange captures the sunlight into a beam that penetrates the mound to an astounding 19 metres within its dark inner chamber. Yet, we must realise that anything that passes on the horizon where the sun passes will be captured into the internal passage and chamber also. The question is whether it does so or not on the special day of Winter Solstice or any other equinox day or Summer Solstice.

The question is how far other celestial alignments can penetrate the passage? Only something exactly on the same declination of the sun would ensure that it was on the same point on the horizon as the sun.

The moon is the most obvious contender, as in the Carrowkeel and Dowth mounds as this was the true intention to capture the moon as well as the sun. As with all mounds the concept seems to have been to incorporate as many functions as possible lunar, solar or stellar. Keen astronomers will be aware that although the moon's path through the sky is slightly inclined to the sun's path, it will share the same position as the sun at certain times throughout the year. If these crossover pathway points happen on the Winter Solstice then effectively the moon would shine into Newgrange in theory. The effective positions of where this would happen would occur twice over an 18.6 year period. In fact an attempt was made to witness the moon inside Newgrange by an amateur research group in July 2001 and again by another group in 2010 for a lunar eclipse, an event not seen for over 450 years. Although cloud cover had hindered the 2001 operation the full moon was witnessed well within the passage but the 2010 group were disappointed. The exercise though not totally fruitful did bear some intriguing results. The question those less familiar with astronomy must be asking right now is surely there are many things whizzing past in the sky that the passage would capture, planets, moon and or stars? Curiously, there are markings on the roof box that may enlighten us. There are a series of eight markings situated above the roof box of Newgrange which may well be an attempt to track the eight-year cycle of Venus. This would show as a prominent 'wandering' star on the horizon. 'Uriel's Machine' a book by Christopher Knight and Robert Lomas, 2000 has brought this to the attention of others and has done amazing research into Venus at ancient sites. We have already noted that the small stone circle of Stanton Drew was dedicated to the eight-year cycle of Venus.

A feminine Venusian theme is repeated elsewhere in the Boyne Valley depicted by the 'eight markings'. Whether Venus cycles were understood or not, the astronomer architects knew to look at this problematic 'wandering' star and invested some interest in trying to figure it's cycle out. It actually ties in very closely with the metonic cycle of the moon which was clearly understood. Setting these objects aside the most obvious thing to ponder is then, given long enough and constant motion of the heavens, wouldn't a star line up with the passageway? The answer is an obvious yes, but more astounding is the fact that we don't have to look too far. On the Winter Solstice the main theme and purpose that Newgrange was built, the star Sirius is almost exactly on the same declination as the sun.

I am not the first to suggest a Sirius connection to Newgrange, there are several works that do so. Kisma Reidling's book 'Faery-Faith Traditional Wisdom: Codex 1 Irish Cosmology & Faery Glamoury, 2004, page 73, describes an alignment of Sirius the Dog Star and Orion alignments. The author however makes out the monument was aligned to solstice events once the stellar event was obsolete, presumably by Precessional effects. In the 'Ulster Journal of Archaeology Volumes 49-51', 1987, the declination of Sirius is discussed in the epoch 3000 BC alongside Newgrange alignments and spirals. More recently in 'Avebury Cosmos', 2011 Nicholas Mann discusses the specific details of a Sirius alignment but as an exact coincidence. There are many people who have written or discussed the Sirius alignment but I don't know of any that have proposed the alignment as intentional in order to calculate precession. This is the essence of my Newgrange Sirius Precessional Calculator Theory linking the Tri-spiral inside and out as a crude Precessional calculator, and the reason I have explored the position of Sirius.

Sirius and the Tri-spiral is the single most significant fact about Newgrange and should not be overlooked. It should be noted that Sirius, given enough time, would span an area of the sky due to Precession and its normal rising motion. So what does that mean? Simply put, at the time of construction it rises upwards, continuously, each night but also shifts to the left every year, thus it covers an area of the sky, in which the sun rises and is aligned. Again simply stating, if it was near the rising sun's position then it obviously at some point does enter the chamber, just like the sun. It is irrelevant exactly what year BC as the window of opportunity is about 200 years, the important point to note here is that it does. The fact that the 200 year window is around the time Newgrange was built is what matters. For the purpose of this article, I have used computer simulations with exact dates. The inclination in Kisma Reidling's book that Newgrange was solely and purposely aligned to Sirius is what I have picked up on, however I elaborate here extensively, it was not a mere spectacle. That's why I think the Tri-spiral artwork on the entrance stone is aligned to Sirius as a marker before it enters the chamber. I also believe that's why the Tri-spiral appears inside the chamber. It is my belief that the builders attempted to calculate precession using Sirius and the sun though the specifics of dates are arbitrary only relying on the accuracy of planetarium software regarding Sirius. Specifically attributing a date to the Tri-spiral alignment of Sirius is only necessary for the purpose of counting the Precessional rate. The importance of this should not be underestimated; the effect of Precession is all about the rate at which it happens. The stars shift one degree every 72 years, in a wobble of the sky, whereby one complete wobble comprises of approximately 26,000 years.

Sirius is in fact so dramatically close to the same point on the horizon as the sun that this was surely noted if not explored. We need an astronomy program to rewind the stars back to peer into the epoch that Newgrange was constructed. This is due to the effect of precession of the equinoxes and the slow shifting of the stars. The thing is even if Sirius was not exactly on the same point on the horizon give a small number of years later it would be. The notion of the Sirius alignment is further explored later in the Newgrange-Sirius Theory below and may well be the most significant evidence we have of the ancient astronomers who indulged in megalithic construction.

The Newgrange-Sirius Theory Unveiled

This theory may be neat and revealing but it isn't exactly the easiest thing to explain to someone who is not adverse in astronomy. This theory relates directly to Sirius being aligned to the Tri spiral art on the entrance stone and the angle this makes with the Winter Solstice alignment. However the chamber and entrance stone are only famous for this Solstice event, I don't know of any theory relating Sirius aligned to the Tri-Spiral or indeed Precessional calculating. The easiest thing is to say that Newgrange is beautifully aligned to the sunrise on the Winter Solstice. That the beam of light on this morning shines down a very long chamber deliberately intended. Then I'd have to tell you that coincidentally or knowingly the star Sirius happens to be, at the time of construction, almost exactly aligned on the same day, that is, the Winter Solstice just after the sun goes down. As Nicholas Mann makes out in 'Avebury Cosmos', 2011 he favours a coincidence, whereby I truly believe they not only knew about this but set up Newgrange to track and calculate precession. As Sirius rises in this epoch and hits the Tri-spiral, which I believe is their marking for Sirius. Then at some point after that Sirius will enter the chamber and there you see a miniature version of the Tri Spiral, again their marking for Sirius. That much may seem acceptable to you. So they had a star doing the almost same thing as the sun, at some moment in time, big deal they were getting double the value for their monument you might think? Then I have to tell you that there is this wayward drifting of the stars that occurs so very slowly over time, an effect called Precession of the Equinoxes, which will automatically make Sirius by default perfectly aligned one day just as accurate as the beam of sunlight. It will not stay aligned to the Tri-spiral. This I'm afraid is the best I can do to keep the science out of it but it also serves to dampen the achievements or perhaps intentions of the architect astronomers of Newgrange. Even if you get your head around this Precessional drifting of the stars and understand the concepts involved it doesn't explain what these builders were really up to. We are just peering deeper into their intellect with unsatisfactory results. Personally I believe the astronomer's architecture was deliberate to capture this phenomenon.

I believe Newgrange also served as a crude Precessional calculator utilising the star Sirius in this epoch. The thing is once you realize all this, coincidence seems unlikely and the intention of Precessional monitoring seems imminent. Quite simply the Newgrange Sirius theory revolves around the Tri-spiral artwork on the entrance stone. When Sirius rises and first hits that, at whatever year, the ancient architects then kept count in Solar years. The monument is aligned to a yearly solar event so that is an easy task. That's why I believe they used the Solstice at Newgrange, an easy obvious yearly marker. Therefore when Sirius hit the back recess of the chamber they noted this significant end of measurement. They then marked the inside of the chamber with the Tri-spiral Sirius logo to mark the event. In effect The Newgrange Sirius theory is an elaborate Precessional Calculator theory.

Firstly there is the fact that they would have been observing at the Newgrange site for many years or generations I should say, marking out their alignments and intentions. They had plenty of time to notice Sirius being where it was on this special day. If you were smart enough to build a huge monument like Newgrange in order to capture a beam of sunlight on the shortest day of the year to such accuracy, then you would have noticed on that same evening that Sirius one of the brightest stars was in the same position, considering you also watched the stars. The Question isn't; did they know all this? It is more like, at what point did they notice this? They looked for stuff in the sky worth noting, worthy of exploring. Regardless whether they knew about the Precession of the Equinoxes before they built their mound or whilst it was newly constructed, they sure knew about it at some point eventually. The fact is they were all about the stars, the constellations, solar and lunar phenomenon, and just about every facet of observational astronomy one can achieve with the naked eye. I think they also had Dowth and the heliacal rising of the Pleiades on the Summer Solstice as another line of investigation into Precessional knowledge, and most likely this avenue of investigation predated Newgrange research. Nothing ever seems accidental about anything they did at these monuments. In 3200 BC we only see a few of degrees difference in the Winter Solstice Sunrise and Sirius rising later that evening as depicted by the Stellarium computer simulations depicted below.

The Newgrange Winter Solstice Sunrise in 3200 BC at Azimuth 135° (Southeast)

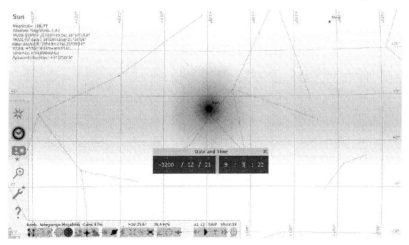

The Newgrange Winter Solstice Evening in 3200 BC: Sirius Rising
at Azimuth 138°

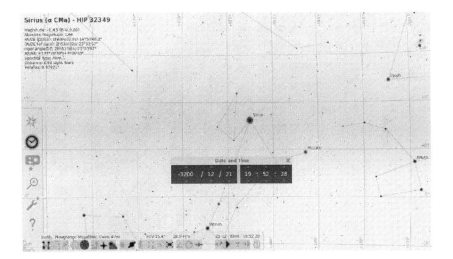

Secondly when you get the lunar and solar knowledge they had and notice other deep cycles like the effect of precession, it seems natural and obvious they would have took this on too. I think they had a lot of essential cosmology already figured out, as anyone can see by their achievements but I think they also had experimental work going on alongside their many efforts. After mapping lunar and solar cycles, they were using these concepts to figure out deeper cycles of time. If I were doing what they were and I noticed this effect of Precession, I would put a marker on a star or constellation and see how long it took to drift a certain amount. They did it for the moon and sun, so why not the stars? I believe this is exactly what they have done on the entrance stone. I am not the first to suggest a theory for the triple spiral artwork, at present there are 26 in total possible interpretations for the Newgrange Entrance stone and its famous tri spiral. The triple spiral is not an abstract symbol for Sirius as it may first seem.

The Newgrange Entrance Stone depicting the famous Tri-Spiral art to the left of the central Winter Solstice line

The Tri-spiral artwork is actually a double spiral with a single spiral attached to it, thus comprising of three spirals. The double spiral is considered in artwork interpretations to be the Equinox symbol. I believe the extra spiral is attached for the Star Sirius adjacent to the double spiral equinox symbol. My interpretation is that this Tri-spiral is showing the Precession of Sirius, that is through the effect of Precession of the Equinox (hence the Double spiral). Speaking in more descriptive terms; Single Spiral (Sirius) is Precessing with the Double spiral (Equinox). If you take all that to be true then you would expect to see this artwork inside, which in fact we do. What is important is not fixating the star Sirius to any specific date; we are fixating it to the Tri-spiral and counting Solar years. We are calculating a rate of precession. This can be so many degrees per year in modern terms. For the megalithic builders they measured from the Tri-spiral to the central line on the entrance stone, in so many years. The central line on the entrance stone is aligned to the winter solstice sunrise.

Sirius apart from being revered by many ancient cultures is in fact a triple star system, of which the Dogon tribe in West Africa are fully knowledgeable on this issue. The Dogon also use the exact same spirals in their symbology. They also use 'sun wheels' exactly like those that occur at other megalithic sites in Ireland, namely Loughcrew and Dowth. Their whole mythology and celestial lore is based around the Star Sirius and the Pleiades constellation, which also occurs at nearby Dowth. The fact that these commonalities exist beg serious explanations. The Dogon did actually march across the top of North Africa from Ancient Egypt to their resting place in Mali. In doing so they were in close proximity to the similar Alcalar Passage Grave Complex of Portugal. The North African journey by sea across the straits of Gibraltar would have been nothing for the megalithic builders who were also skilled mariners. This is only one suggestion I have to put forward how this interconnecting symbolism being related to one another by a transfer of Knowledge. The passage grave builders were in close proximity to the Dogon's migration as they themselves had traversed the coastline of South Western Europe. They both possessed such similar knowledge from the same epoch; perhaps there was a trade of information? Perhaps they had the same teachers or knowledge givers?

The Newgrange Sirius Winter Solstice Alignment of 3000 BC, Azimuth 135°

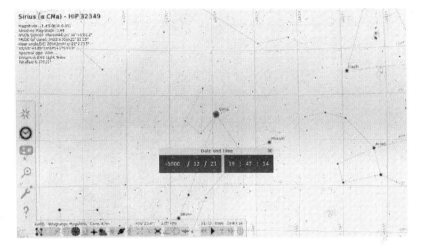

The neat thing is that if the Triple spiral on the entrance stone does represent the Sirius alignment, it would be in just the right place that you would put a marker. The straight line that marks the sun on the centre of the stone is given as the Winter Solstice marker. It still occurs today for all to see. At around the time of construction Sirius would rise up and hit to the left of this central line. Eventually the star rising year after year closer and closer until it hit the centre of the entrance stone. In doing so it would naturally hit the inner chamber too. As mentioned eariler, a miniature version of the entrance stone Tri Spiral occurs inside the back recess chamber and nowhere else at Newgrange. I have shown an exact alignment of Sirius and Newgrange in 3000 BC. The mathematical analysis given below at the time it hit the centre of the triple spiral would be approximately 3070 BC, approximately one degree of precession later it hits the inner chamber. This can be calculated using trigonometry, knowing the length of the chamber and the distance from Tri Spiral to the Winter Solstice centre line thus making a triangle.

Math Analysis for the Newgrange Precessional Calculator Theory

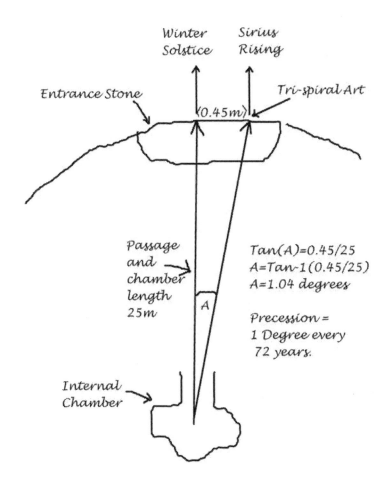

Newgrange Precessional Calculator.

Winter Solstice Sirius Rising

Entrance Stone Tri-spiral Art

(0.45m)

Passage and chamber length 25m

A

$Tan(A)=0.45/25$
$A=Tan-1(0.45/25)$
$A=1.04\ degrees$

Precession =
1 Degree every
72 years.

Internal Chamber

Newgrange may be a crude Precessional calculator by today's measurement techniques, but of the era it was built it was highly sophisticated, some may argue it still is. If you started counting the years from the time Sirius struck the Tri Spiral Art, until it hit the

Winter Solstice marker you would effectively have a rate of precession. If you refuse to accept that the Tri-spiral on the entrance stone is Sirius, you are still left with the fact that Sirius rose and hit the centre of it. My analysis and entrance stone artwork theory is the only one that explains the presence of the Tri Spiral inside the Newgrange chamber as Sirius also migrated inside. It may also explain why Newgrange fell out of use, as it had done its duty. In my years of research I had also come across the Temple of Denderah in Egypt. It too like Newgrange was aligned to Sirius in the same epoch; Sirius being so bright was used to light up the central passageway at night time. There is also evidence to show that Denderah temple was previous built slightly off angle, and was realigned because precession had naturally misaligned it over the centuries.

This theory boasts strong astronomical evidence, rich artwork and symbology and is fitting with other Sirius worshipping civilizations of the same epoch. Many other ancient civilizations around the world seem to have attempted to calculate the rate of Precession, an anomaly of ancient history yet to be explained.

www.jamesswagger.com

www.capricornmembers.com

Ballyalban Ring Fort

From the accurate astronomical alignments to the legends of old, Ireland is rich in places steeped in myth and magic. Ballyalban Ring Fort dates back to the Druid Iron Age. Ireland's Fairy Forts or ring forts are said to be the remains of strongholds and other dwellings. Local tradition holds that fairies make their home in these ring forts and bad luck will come to anyone who tries to destroy them. Although these beliefs only date back to the 12th century, they were strong enough to allow thousands of ring forts to avoid destruction as land was being extensively cultivated.

Ballyalban Ring Fort has been preserved for a legendary reason. Local country lore says that it guarded by a pooka in the shape of a pony. Pookas are said to ne malevolent fairies which take the shape of animals.

Faeries are said to populate wooden glens. A visit to the Glen, a tiny valley which is tucked into Knocknerea Mountain in Sligo, Ireland, is a must. This living mountain is home to many sacred sites, including a possible passage tomb at its base. The Glen also contains an atmospheric stone cairn that legend calls the grave of Queen Maeve, a powerful female figure from Irish Mythology, often equated a with Queen Mab of the fairies.

The cairn of Queen Maeve's Tomb

The Element of Water

To the Celts, water was sacred. Springs, rivers, lakes and the seas were seen as entrances to the Otherworld. Many vortex offerings have been found in the rivers as the Odines, the spirits of the water, were seen as helpful beings. One of the most visually spectacular expressions of water is a waterfall. Rich in energy their power can be felt and heard. When we attune to these locations, we are connecting with the power of water - water is the life force on Earth - without it there would be no growth, no life.

Glen Brittle Forest, Isle of Skye

Glen Brittle Forest on the Isle of Skye boasts beautiful waterfalls that can only be reached by hiking. It is worth the walk as you will be captivated by their natural beauty and these so-called Fairy Pools in unspoilt isolated areas are breathtaking and naturally reconnect us to Nature.

A Fairy Pool on the Isle of Skye.

Similarly, the welcoming and invigorating waterfall in Cornwall called **St. Nectan's Kieve, near Boscastle, Cornwall,** with its rock basins and arches, is associated with otherworldly fairies that inspire visitors to create shrines out of ribbons, rocks and crystals. Nearby, in the traditional Cornish town of Boscastle is the Witches Museum which is a real hidden gem and a must for the open-minded.

The Giant's Ring, Belfast, Ireland.

Just on the outskirts of the bustling city of Belfast stands The Giant's Ring. With a Spirit of Place that is ever present, this monument stands out as it is very unusual. A huge circular earthen bank some 3.5 metres high enclosing a sacred space some 180 metres in diameter   and   2.8   hectares   in   area.

At least three of the 5 irregularly-spaced gaps in the henge are original. At the esoteric centre and heart of the enclosure is a small yet impressive passage-tomb that once faced west towards the setting equinox sunset. Excavations beyond the bank yielded evidence of Neolithic activity. Walking on the bank and looking down into the enclosure will give you a sense of drama and space. Did spectators once stand upon the bank and watch ceremonies or events carried out below?

Tombs for the dead?

I have said that the so-called passage tombs were originally sacred spaces used for initiation, oracle chambers or healing spaces. Burials were the secondary use of the site, and so we can visualise this sacred space as a ceremonial focus point. Converging and emerging at this point are earth energies making a geodetic power centre- one of the strongest in Northern Ireland.

Situated on an elevated plateau, the ring brings you closer to the skies to heaven itself. When walking upon the bank, I got the distinct impression that the stone setting faced west because the enclosure becomes alive at, and after, sunset. Imagine the setting sun casting red and golden hues across the open sky. On this Quarter Day, when day and night are of equal length, perhaps ancient people waited for the Moon to rise and shine her pale light upon the land and its people. It's tempting to think that a priest bid farewell to the solar energy of the setting sun whilst a priestess received the energies of the rising Moon. Once the open horizon line was defined by the earthen circle making a natural astronomical amphitheatre.

Nobody really knows what happened in this vast open circle, yet I always sense a yin-yang balance. As I watched the last rays of the setting sun cast its pale golden light, I was reminded of the Golden Age of millennia ago, and so I whispered, 'Come again', to those wise old stones and left feeling uplifted. To my surprise and delight, as I walked away I realised a large bright waxing moon had been watching me. These events touch our hearts as divine connections and synchronicities weave their magic into our lives. I am sure that you have had your own personal experiences at these power places - aren't they magical giving us a sense of pure wonder.

Oweynagat - A portal to the Otherworld

Pure wonder is in plenty that this site. It is so amazing that you will be changed by its silent and ever present power. Oweynagat is also known as the 'Cave of Cats' and it is one of the most evocative, strange and transformative sites I have ever encountered. Oweynagat is a mystifying souterrain, a bit like the fogous' of Cornwall, as it takes you inside of the Earth and inside of yourself.

At first glance, this sacred site looks like a cave but it has a two-metre passageway which you have to crawl along, then you will encounter a dark and descending passageway, as the floor slopes downward for a further 8 metres into a naturally formed cave. This description is true and accurate but it cannot prepare you for the feeling you get in the so-called 'cave'. After crawling along the damp and often muddy sloping corridor, that is a tight squeeze, suddenly it open up into a cathedral like room to call it a cave robs this sacred space of her ageless beauty. I followed author E.A. James Swagger into this site and we had read descriptions, but neither one of us was ready for the 'cave'. Instantly, we were silenced by the feeling, the room's power and we just looked around in awe. James loves to sound tone and the reverb was magical.

The cave has some worked stone that gives it a sense of grandeur which is around 20 metres in length and 6 metres high. Silent and still, this inner chamber really does make you feel that you are in the womb of Gaia or in the Otherworld.

Ogham writing A lintel supports the entrance which is magnificent as it has Ogham writing on it, which is shown in the photograph, and reproduced with kind permission from E.A. James Swagger of **www.megalithicodyssey.com**. The Ogham writing states that 'Fraech, Son of Medb', but it is impossible accurately date it to any given era.

Oweynagat features in Irish mythology, because it is located near Queen Medb's fort which was at the esoteric centre of the ancient Connaught capital of 'Cruachan'. To ancient peoples the esoteric centre or 'navel' of the land was a powerful concept. The centre of the land was the focal point of its sacred energy, the place where the soul or genii of the locale resided. In ancient China Peking was placed at the centre of the Chinese landscape in the same way that an English manor house or stately home stands at the centre of its landscape. Throughout the ancient world the geospiral pattern which was mentioned earlier marked the esoteric centre of a temple, stone circle or pyramid. Constantly emitting harmonious energy, it imbues the site or building with life-enhancing energy. Generated by a underground yin water the geospiral pattern was revered throughout the ancient world. Geodetic dowsers consider it the most powerful form of earth energy which I have studied for over 20 years.

Birth and Rebirth

The cave 's holy history links to birth and rebirth as it is said to be the birthplace of Queen Medb. Legend recalls that a goddess and fairy queen named Étain was fleeing her human husband with her fairy lover Midir. Midir wished to visit a relative named Sinech (meaning 'large-breasted one') who lived in the cave, which was said to be a great palace in the otherworld. A maidservant named Crochan Crogderg (meaning 'blood-red cup') became besotted with the place and was granted the cave by Étian. Crochan gave birth to a daughter, Medb in the confines of the cave.

Originally, the cave had two entrances, although one entrance has collapsed. In Celtic times, you probably left through the now blocked entrance; so you actually journeyed through the dark passageway, into the otherworld, the mesmerising cave and then your ascent begins through the passageway of the other entrance and back into the light of day.

Certainly, you enter in one state and leave feeling differently as if reborn or changed within the womb of Gaia.

Myths and tales of the Morrigan

Many different myths from the lifetime of Medb surround the cave, some say it is a portal through which the Morrigan used to pass to the otherworld. The Morrigan was the goddess of war and strive and was said to drive her otherworldly cattle into the cave at Oweynagat each sunset. Once she stole the herds of a girl named Odras and brought them with her to the otherworld. Odras tried to follow Morrigan but was turned into a lake by the goddess.

Yet another story tells us that 'Ellen Trechen' was a three headed monster that emerged from the cave and ravaged the local countryside before being killed by the Ulaid poet and hero Amergin.

Another legend says that one of Medb's male servants called Nera met a fairy woman in the cave and married her. His fairy bride warned that Medb's palace would be burnt to the ground the following Samhain (November 1st) by creatures from the otherworld. Responding Medb stationed all her forces in the cave at Samhain to protect it from harm. Certainly, this sacred space has an aura of protection and sanctity.

For centuries, the cave continued to be known as portal to the otherworld and oral tradition says that around Samhain its power is greatest. At this time of the solar year the veil between this world and the Otherworld grows thin. However, as Christianity took hold in Ireland, the belief in the cave being a 'gateway to hell' grew as recorded in an 18th century religious text that describes Oweynagat as the 'hell-mouth of Ireland'. It was believed that Oweynagat was linked to another 'hell-mouth' many miles away at the Kesh Corran.

The Hill of Tara

The Hill of Tara was once the ancient seat of power in Ireland. Crowning the hilltop, 142 kings are said to have reigned there in prehistoric and medieval times.

In ancient Irish mythology, Tara also known as Temair was a sacred place, a dwelling for the gods, and believed to be an entrance to the Otherworld. In a way, Tara is the seat of Irish pagan power, so it comes as no surprise that Saint Patrick is said to have come to Tara to confront the ancient pagan religion at its most powerful site.

One interpretation of the name Tara says that it means a *place of great prospect* and on a clear day it is claimed that features in half the counties of Ireland can be seen from Tara. To the northwest can be seen the brilliant white quartz front of Newgrange and further north lies the Hill of Slane, where according to legend, St. Patrick lit his Pascal fire prior to his visit to Tara in 433 AD.

Early in the 20th century a group of Israelites came to Tara with the conviction that the Arc of the Covenant was buried on the famous hill. Apparently, they dug the Mound of the Synods in search of the Arc but only found some old Roman coins. An archaeological excavation in the 1950s unearthed circles of post holes, suggesting the construction of substantial buildings once stood here. The earliest activity was a Neolithic settlement and the Mound of the Hostages was constructed in the Bronze Age around 2500BC.

Using non-intrusive archaeological techniques and aerial photography, a huge temple measuring 170 metres which was constructed from 300 wooden posts was recently discovered. Only two monuments at Tara have been excavated - The Mound of the Hostages in the 1950s, and the Rath of the Synods at the turn of the 19th-20th Centuries.

Sitting on top of the King's Seat (Forradh) of Temair is the most famous of Tara's monuments - Ireland's ancient coronation stone - the Lia Fail or "Stone of Destiny", which was brought here according to mythology by the Tuatha Dé Danann, which was said to roar when touched by the rightful King of Tara.

The Stone of Destiny was located just north of the Mound of Hostages and it was moved to its current site after the Battle of Tara during the Irish revolution of 1798 to mark the graves of 400 rebels who died here.

Some claim the stone was flat and it was moved from Tara by King Fergus of Scotland and was named the Stone of Scone which then became the coronation stone of British kings at Westminster Cathedral. However, most historians accept that the present granite pillar at Tara is the true Stone of Destiny. Stories abound and one legend states that it was only one of four stones positioned at the cardinal directions on Tara.

In the nearby churchyard at Tara there are two standing stones, which are believed to be the vestiges of a stone monument. The tall stone is said to feature a figure of the Celtic fertility god Cernunnos and is similar to many of the 'Sheela na Gig' symbols found throughout Ireland.

Witness a shadow-line at Avebury

During my

investigations at Avebury Hnege with Busty Taylor, we discovered an intriguing shadow-line that coincided with the Celtic New Year. Samhain (Early November festival) means the 'end of summer' and heralds the darkness of the coming winter. It was the start of the Old Druid year when the gods drew near to the earth, and when the veil to the Otherworld is the thinnest.

At long the the inner this this

sunset the southern portal stones (Devil's Chair and Stone 98) cast a black co-joined shadow, which stretches across the ground in front of causeway entrance and terminates at henge bank. To enter the southern circle one would have to walk across dark shadow-line and we surmise that was an esoteric design feature.

Fortuitously, both megaliths are still in their original positions and you can see this archaic shadow-path today on the 4th-7th November, as the following photograph shows.

I think the shadow line was a part of a lost tradition. The shadow line is very dark and if you stand in it you sense an extraordinary power. I felt intuitively that I was to leave behind my failures, my sorrows, and my misgivings of the year behind. It felt like the dark shadow line was naturally drawing these energies from my being. I realised that a bright light line was in front of me and I was to step from the dark into the light of the Celtic New Year – refreshed and anew.

Ley lines and earth currents

Sacred sites are portals that take us on a journey to raise our consciousness. Ley line connect the sites and are all powerful and sometimes the linear line has yin and yang currents entwining them, a bit like the symbol of healing – the caduceus. Ancient sites can be aligned upon the currents as well as the ley imbuing the site with power. Earth energies can be seen as natural currents in the earth that are like meridian lines, veins and arteries; living energies that are a part of Gaia.

We have seen that Gaia can produce deep inner waters that are so pure that the water is said in esoteric divining lore to have consciousness. If you place a standing stone upon anyone of these living energies, the stone's crystal lattice absorbs the energy and transforms it from earth energy into aerial energy that is transmitted across the countryside.

Rodney Hale and myself have recorded the electromagnetic energy being emitted and transmitted by the stones. The energy lines emitted by the stones are a reality and I believe the electromagnetic energy was harnessed by our ancestors. Theories abound but what is important is your own personal experience of a sacred site as it has the power to change you in many, many ways. Silent alchemy of the soul gently and naturally occurs in these power places. Trust your intutuion and inner guidance to where you should be within a sacred site and follow your heart.

Experience the Earth Force
Let us now see the hidden earth energies were integrated into the Celtic landscape of Uffington Castle in Oxfordhire.

The Uffington White Horse complex

Many diverse leys and earth energies can be experienced in the legendary landscape of Uffington which is steeped in myths and

Arthurian tales.

Dragon Hill

According to the 17th century antiquarian John Aubrey Dragon Hill is the tumulus of Uther

Pendragon, King Arthur's father. 'That Uther Pendragon fought against the Saxons is certayne: perhaps was here slayne, from whence Dragon Hill may take its denomination.'

I have mentioned that a ley line can have a yin and yang line coiling around. This is a ley system. Often the meandering rivers of energy are called Dragon lines which are are male/solar and female/lunar serpentine currents and where they cross is considered especially auspicious.

Uffington Castle

Uffington Castle is classified as an Iron Age hill fort but it certainly was not built to be defensive and so is more likely to have been a Druidic ceremonial centre. Gary Biltcliffe and Caroline Hoare discovered that the Elen dragon current coursed through the causeway entrances. Belinus, the male dragon current, enters through the ramparts and crosses Elen at the near centre.

A Genesis ley

There is another form of earth energy called a Genesis ley which is a hermaphrodite line where male and female energies flow harmoniously together as one imbuing the area with balancing and harmonic energy.

My late father discovered that Genesis energy lines emerge from one location and flow across the landscape for a short distance, or sometimes several miles, before descending into the ground and terminating. They can meander like a river or be relatively straight and their characteristic feature is that they emerge from the ground and form two-ram horn spirals which are highly energizing. One is clockwise, the other counter-clockwise; they are male and female vortices forming a distinctive serpent tail. One sacred site may be associated with the emerging energy, another with the descending energy and several sacred sites may be positioned along the hermaphrodite line.

Dragon Hill

Dragon's hill's summit is sculptured flat and was once used for ceremonial activity. It is one of the most powerful places to experience a Genesis line. On the hill's summit a Genesis ley emerges from two 'ram-horn spirals', the yin and yang vortices are powerful and cause a dowsing rod to spin wildly. The line flows to Wayland's Smithy where it enters a burial chamber.

The Uffington White Horse

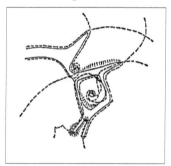

According to Guy Underwood the horse's head was once a dragon head with 'dragon horns' which he dowsed in the 1950s.

Ancient wisdom can be applied to a modern generation. By adopting old geomantic practices we can spiritualize our homes and workspaces. Divining the hidden geodetic signature of our home or locality allows us to understand its energy and reveals why people become ill in certain houses or why certain businesses flourish. Location is all-important. Future building projects could implement geomantic awareness and create constructs which will benefit and serve humanity whilst living in harmony with Gaia's energies. Schools, offices and our homes could benefit from geodetic decodement whilst avoiding geopathic stress zones.

My passion is to show people the power of Earth's energy system so that we can return to living in harmony with the Earth. Sacred sites show us this.

Wayland's Smithy long barrow]

The Genesis line that emerged from Dragon Hill courses along the barrow's axis. My late father discovered that it pulses in 7 places which are the barrow's chakras. It descends into the far chamber which marks the Crown Chakra.

I believe that ancient wisdom can be applied to a modern generation. By adopting old geomantic practices we can spiritualize our homes and workspaces. Divining the hidden geodetic signature of our home or locality allows us to understand its energy and reveals why people become ill in certain houses or why certain businesses flourish. Location is all-important. Future building projects could implement geomantic awareness and create constructs which will benefit and serve humanity whilst living in harmony with Gaia's energies. Schools, offices and our homes could benefit from geodetic decodement whilst avoiding geopathic stress zones.

My passion is to show people the power of Earth's energy system so that we can return to living in harmony with the Earth. Sacred sites show us this.

If you would like to contact me for a tour please go to www.theaveburyexperience.co.uk or if you would like to study dowsing and other esoteric subjects go to www.EsotericCollege.com or you can email me at mariawheatley@aol.com